Data Warehousing and Decision Support

—The State of the Art, Volume 2

SPECIAL OFFER TO READERS

Order more copies of this book, or any SPIRAL Book, at a 20% discount plus shipping & handling.

<u>How to redeem this offer:</u>

- Complete the information below and <u>fax</u> this page to 603-647-1977
- Or, call 1-800-SPIRALL (800-774-7255) and mention "offer dw20"
- Or, order on-line at http://www.spiralbooks.com
- Or, complete this form and mail to:

SPIRAL BOOKS

Stark Mill Building, Suite 401, 500 Commercial Street, Manchester, NH 03101-1151
tel: 603-647-2344 fax: 603-647-1977

ITEMS ORDERED ($36 each, plus $5 S&H for first item):

[ ] DW, volume 2 [ISBN1-57109-010-X]: $36 each, plus $5 S&H for first item

[ ] DW, volume 1 [ISBN1-57109-005-3]: $36 each, plus $5 S&H for first item

When available in 1997:

[ ] Internet & Data Warehousing— More than Meets the Eye [ISBN1-57109-007-X]

[ ] Internet Tools— Building the Infrastructure [ISBN1-57109-011-8]

[ ] The Internet &Electronic Commerce— EDI, EFT, & Beyond [ISBN1-57109-012-6]

[ ] Data Across the Intranet [ISBN1-57109-009-6]

[ ] PLACE me on the SPIRAL Books mailing list

[ ] CONTACT me when new books become available

[ ] CONTACT me about placing a white paper in a SPIRAL Book

[ ] CONTACT me about DW & DS consulting services for my organization

Bill To/Ship To Contact (use a separate page for other shipping address):

Address:

Phone (required): _____   Fax: _____

Choose one: [ ] Mastercard   [ ] VISA   [ ] Discover   [ ] AMEX

Charge card #: _____   Exp. Date: _____

Name as it appears on the card: _____

Signature: _____

Data Warehousing and Decision Support

—The State of the Art, Volume 2

Compiled by The SPIRAL Group

Foreword by William Juch

Pam Roth, Program Director

SPIRAL BOOKS

Data Warehousing and Decision Support
—The State of the Art, Volume 2
by The SPIRAL Group

Acquisitions Editor: Pam Roth

SPIRAL Books
are published by SPIRAL Communications, Inc.

Library of Congress Catalog Card Number: 95-69148

ISBN 1-57109-010-x

Cover Design by Camino Design
Layout by The SPIRAL Group

To communicate with The SPIRAL Group, or for information about other SPIRAL Books, contact:

SPIRAL Books
Stark Mill Building, Suite 401
500 Commercial Street
Manchester, NH 03101-1151
tel: 603-647-2344
fax: 603-647-1977
spiral29@idt.mainstream.net
www.spiralbooks.com

Dedication

To Luke

...the best dog a Pam could have

Acknowledgments

We wish to thank the following people and organizations for their support:

Roberta Carleton, Neal Hill, Cognos, Inc.

Valerie Moser, Erin McGinnis, Lois Richards, Dynamic Information Systems Corporation (DISC)

Tiffany Lorello, Michael J. Saylor, MicroStategy, Inc.

David Butler, NCR, Inc.

Lisa Goldberg, Lisa Roche, PLATINUM *technology, inc.*

Doug Prouty, Gareth Taube, Joel Klebanoff, Praxis International Inc.

Debbie Benoit, Doug Laney, Prism Solutions, Inc.

Cindy Mayron, Mike Olson, Red Brick Systems, Inc.

William Juch, Pam Roth, The SPIRAL Group

Credits

Cover Design by Camino Design

Logo by Gordon Design

On-line Logo by Warburton Design

Book Layout by The SPIRAL Group

Contents

Foreword

We have come a long way since the first volume of **Data Warehousing and Decision Support** was published in 1995. Since then, a number of predictions made by The SPIRAL Group in the study **The Role of Data Warehousing in MIS** have come to pass.

First, Windows NT Server has become a viable platform for data warehousing. In 1997, over 30% of data marts, subject-oriented data warehouses, or departmental data warehouses will run on NT Server. NT won't replace Unix in this role, nor will it replace the exciting new generation of small foot print, high performance mainframes from IBM and Unisys, to name a few. But NT has a solid following in the data mart role. This is the proper role for NT, until we see it more able to scale.

A second trend has been for companies to concentrate on projects with a high likelihood of success. Predictably successful projects include projects that can be implemented in less than 12 months. These projects include building departmental data marts, building subject-oriented data warehouses and using decision support tools running against replicated production data bases. Leading vendors like NCR have come up with soup-to-nuts data warehouse programs that guarantee, under certain conditions, a successful implementation within a certain time frame, at an agreed on or fixed cost.

A third trend has been the continuing use of mainframes for strategic data analysis. For storing, retrieving, and crunching large amounts of information, the mainframe still has no peer. In arenas like pharmaceuticals and health care, legacy systems will retain and expand their utility as firms drill down into historical data to predict health trends, target potential problem areas all in an effort to manage costs. The Health Care Act of 1996 will put even more pressure on this area.

We've found that a large part of the process of implementing a successful data warehouse is in the cleaning of data and meta-data in order to establish a system of record. Clients report spending a majority of their time and effort in data cleansing before the data warehouse is loaded. As more departments or legacy systems are brought into the project, this process gets more complex. Look for consultants and tools that have a track record in this area. Investments here have payback for operational systems, too.

There is probably no area where a multiple tier architecture makes more sense than in the realm of strategic data analysis. A multi-tier architecture gives the most flexibility, analysis potential, and scalability. Simply, a data warehouse server, an analysis engine (such as that from MicroStrategy) or data mart, and client decision support applications should be the default architecture that most enterprises consider from the beginning of their project. Too much time, I fear, has been spent on arcane discussions of data models rather than looking at data cleansing, strategic business requirements, and multi-tier architectures.

Don't be afraid to write your own customer care or decision support applications in order to achieve competitive advantage. Benchmarking and relying on best practices alone makes you no better than the next guy.

William Juch,
The SPIRAL Group
Manchester, NH
March 1997

Chapter 1

The Heart of a Data Warehouse: A Dynamic Environment

Why a Real Data Warehouse Must Be Scaleable

—NCR, Inc.

Introduction

To fully understand data warehousing, it is important to understand the end-to-end nature of the data warehousing process. But of all the framework components, one element stands out in importance: Between getting data into the warehouse from operational systems and getting information out of the warehouse from tools and applications lays "The Heart of the Data Warehouse."

In this paper, we will describe those key dimensions that must be considered when evaluating what the "heart" should look like and how it can perform the functions required of it.

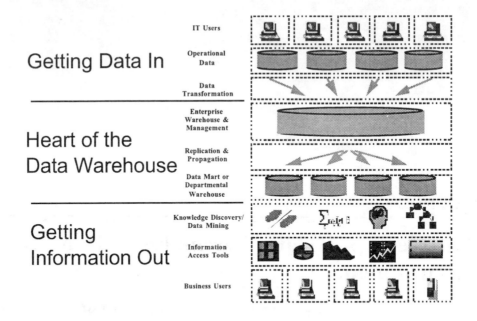

Figure 1: A Scaleable Data Warehouse Framework

At the heart of any data warehouse is the data that represents your business. As this white paper will show, this data is dynamic. It changes as the business grows. It changes as the operational data changes. It changes as the business questions change. It changes as the number of users change. It changes as the applications change. It changes as the tools used to access the data change. In fact, you will see that there is very little that doesn't change in a real production data warehouse.

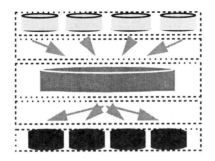

Figure 2: The Heart of the Data Warehouse

If a warehouse is built around a database engine that can not handle the dynamic nature of your data at the heart of the warehouse, failure often follows. Either users are limited in the questions they can ask; or the data being queried becomes days or even weeks or months old; or separate independent systems need to be built, severely limiting the cross-functional nature of the business questions that can be asked; or summary data is used instead of detail. In short, the business value is severely reduced and companies give up on data warehousing all together.

To examine the "heart of the Data Warehouse," we begin with the fundamentals: "data" and "queries". We look at how data is organized and used, and infer from that just what requirements data warehousing places on the database engine. Then, we cover the differences between summary and detail data. Finally, we cover how the data is used in data warehousing—specifically, we discuss "the query." We differentiate between simple and complex queries, as well as between pre-defined and ad-hoc queries.

The white paper concludes with a discussion of just what all of this means for "scalability" in the data warehouse environment.

Data Organization

What is at the heart of the data warehouse?

The answer is very simple: It is your data about your business. It can include every aspect of doing business with the outside world: finance, accounting, logistics, etc. Or it may start out with a subset of your business. It is data about what is going on today, and it is a record of what has happened in the past. A fundamental key to understanding what data warehousing does and how you can benefit from it is to understand how this data is organized.

It should come as no surprise that your data is organized in a way that represents your business. And in the Relational Database model, this means the data exists not as a single, huge file of rows and columns, but as a collection of <u>tables</u> that use the "row and column" model.

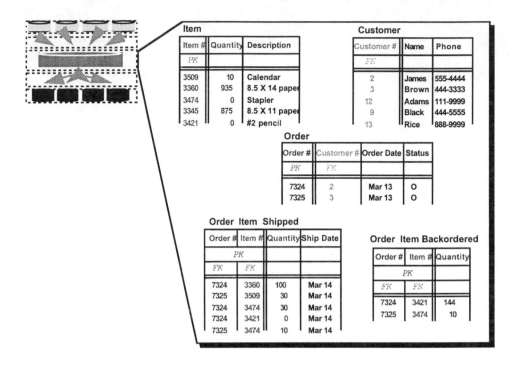

Figure 3: The Data Model = The Business Model

Here is a simple example of how data would be organized for an office supplies company. In this example, there is an order table, a customer table, a shipping table, and so on. While the information to fill these tables may come from different operational systems, within the data warehouse this is how the data is organized.

This chart is the key to understanding relational tables. The point is that the tables are interrelated. Every table is tied to at least one other table through interrelated columns.

For example, look at the "Item" table. The first column, "Item #," is also present in two other tables: "Order Item Shipped" and "Order Item Backordered." The color coding in this chart shows how all tables are similarly interrelated through other columns.

Now that we see how your data is organized, let's walk through examples of how it is used. The two primary categories for using relational databases are On Line Transaction Processing (OLTP) or Decision Support (DSS).

You will see that these two kinds of database usage are very different and create very different demands on the underlying database engine.

Transaction Processing

We illustrate transaction processing with a simple example: a customer wants to place an order. In this case, Mr. Brown orders a calendar. This is traditional "on-line transaction processing" or OLTP.

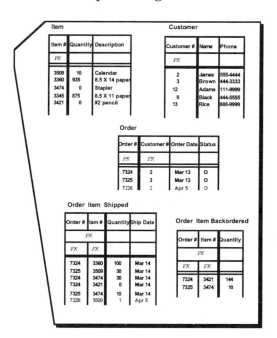

Figure 4: OLTP

1. A new order is opened on the Order table, so the next order number is used— in this case, #7326. The Order table is filled out, including Brown's customer number and the date the order was placed.

2. We go to the Shipping table. The system knows you just opened order #7326, because the two columns are "keyed" together (interrelated). So the user inserts the product number for the calendar (#3509), the quantity shipped (1), and the date to ship. The transaction is now complete.

This example transaction demonstrates three key things:

1. Of all the tables available (and there will be many, many more), the transaction only touches a few of them.

2. The transaction did not have to scan any tables, some of which could have billions of rows, and

3. There was very little IO or processing involved.

These three things typify the OLTP environment. Notice how relatively simple the requirements for OLTP are. The OLTP database engines on the market today were designed for maximum efficiency in this "quick-in, quick-out" computing environment.

Decision Support Processing

We now take a look at the other way to use your data: Decision Support.

In this example, a business user wants to find the answer to a specific question about the company's pencil customers so he can target them for a promotion. In particular, the query is "Which customers placed the majority of their orders for pencils in the first quarter of the year?"

The first thing to notice about this usage that immediately sets it apart from the OLTP environment is that many tables have to be scanned as the first step towards getting the answer.

Figure 5 shows how all the tables are needed to begin answering this query. We start with finding the part number for pencils in the "Item" table. Then we start scanning the "Order Item Shipped" table for that part number. When we find an order that includes pencils, we see how many were shipped in that order. In this case, none were shipped. But since the order was opened, it must mean that we didn't have the pencils in inventory. So we proceed to the "Order Item Backordered" table for the quantity that the customer ordered. Once we find the quantity, we have to determine who ordered them— after all, that was the basis of the question— and to do that, we refer to the "Order" table to find out which customer placed the order. We find out that it was customer #2. We then have to go to the "Customer" table to identify who that customer was.

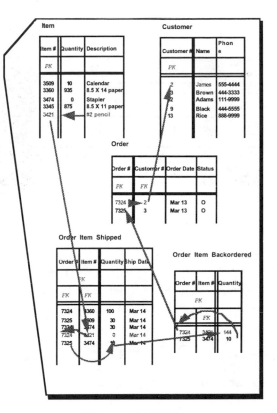

Figure 5: DSS

OLTP vs. DSS

All of this bouncing around between tables is very different from OLTP.

The second thing that differentiates DSS from OLTP is that we do not just "pop in and out" of these tables: we have to do massive searches through them, sometimes multiple times. This is a huge IO intensive task, and can take a lot of time.

The last thing that differentiates these two operating environments is that after all of the data necessary for answering the question is gathered, it has to be put together properly. This involves things like aggregations, joins, sorts, conditional requirements like "if-then" statements, etc. All of these things are very processor intensive.

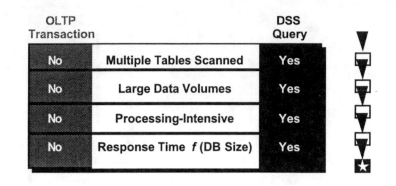

OLTP Transaction		DSS Query
No	Multiple Tables Scanned	Yes
No	Large Data Volumes	Yes
No	Processing-Intensive	Yes
No	Response Time f (DB Size)	Yes

Figure 6: OLTP vs. DSS

The point is that, if we view OLTP transactions and DSS queries side by side, we see just how dramatically different they are. OLTP is "quick-in, quick-out." By comparison, DSS queries can take a long time to complete, depending on all sorts of specifics about what is being asked.

To summarize this first section of "The Heart of the Data Warehouse," your data is stored in the form of multiple tables. These tables model your business. On-line transaction processing systems do not scan many of these tables at once, and they don't access large data volumes. This keeps them from being processor and IO intensive, and keeps their response time from being significantly affected by the size of the database.

Decision Support systems are just the opposite. They usually do full scans of multiple tables, which involves reading very large amounts of data and makes them processing-intensive. Since processing times are a function of data volume, the responsiveness of decision support systems is heavily affected by the size of the database involved.

Summary vs. Detail Data

Now that we have covered how your data is organized and used, and how that usage affects the requirements on the database engine, we take a closer look at the data itself.

Figure 7 is an example of what detail vs. summary data looks like. On the left hand side, we have the detailed scanner data being produced as the transactions happen. This is every item sold at every moment of every day.

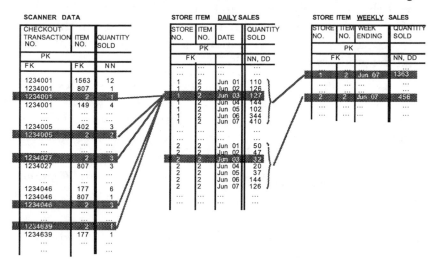

Figure 7: Summary Data

In the middle, we have the first pass at summarization. This takes away the clarity of the detail. Instead of knowing which items sold at which store at which hour of the day, now the data is simply summarized into daily sales by store. On the right, we have the next level of summarization where we can see only how many of each unit were sold by each store each week.

Summarization can occur at many levels. The point is, when you summarize data, you hide valuable information. For example, if the only data available to business users was "unit volume by week," how could you determine the effectiveness of a special promotion that occurred on Tuesday and Wednesday? The answer is hidden in the detail, and the user can't know how effective the promotion was.

With summary data, you simply cannot get answers to basic questions like:

- What is the daily sales pattern for item 2 at any store?
- When item 2 is purchased, what is most frequently purchased with it?
- What is the profile of a typical customer who buys item 2?

Summary data has strong limitations regarding its informational value. As Figure 7 shows, summary data can't answer the question about daily sales patterns by store. It can't explain what else was purchased in the same market basket, and it can't tell you anything about what kind of customer purchased the product.

Summary data can only give you summary answers, which only allows you to be reactive. In this example, it would make the retailer slow to find "out-of-stock" situations, and miss revenue opportunity as a result. Or, he would find out too late that he was overstocked— a discovery that would force him to hold a "blue light special" promotion.

Only detailed data can answer these very basic questions. And with detailed data, you can find detailed answers. This allows you to move away from being reactive and move toward being proactive.

For example, if this retailer can use the detail to find out which products tend to sell together in the same market basket, he might change the layout of his shelf display systems to encourage this kind of buying. Or, if he can find out what type of customer is buying a particular product or grouping of products, he can target a specialized promotion that may cross-sell that user on other items.

Given the significant business limitations associated with summary data, you may ask why summary data is so popular. The answer lies in the past. For decades, data has been held in a summarized form for several very good reasons.

1. To shrink the volume of data so the database engine can handle it. In the past, database engines could not handle the volumes associated with detail data.

2. To shrink the volume of data in order to reduce storage costs. In the past, the cost of storing a Terabyte was astronomical.

3. To shrink the volume of data in order to reduce MIPS requirements. In the past, only mainframes could do the compute intensive work associated with DSS, and mainframe MIPS prices were astronomical.

4. To improve the performance of predefined processing tasks. In the past, most companies were not concerned with automating responses to sudden changes in the business. This implied that the questions to be answered by a decision support system were known ahead of time. All

they needed was the traditional, high-level reporting, such as weekly or monthly reports.

In other words, summarization is a technique from an old paradigm— one where technology prices were exorbitant, the technology was extremely limited in its capabilities, and where companies were not forced to be proactive in responding to sudden changes in their business. In today's competitive world, this old paradigm will no longer lead to business success.

Many customers in many industries have discovered the value of detailed data. One data warehouse user summed it up this way: "Summary data leads to averaged data which leads to average answers which leads to average decisions, which leads to average performance." He pointed out that his company could not afford to be an average performer.

Of course, summary data still has its place in a Data Warehouse. Organizing logical or physical "Data Marts" can provide quick response to predefined questions. This can be very valuable. But if a company is trying to get back to intimate relationships with their customers and suppliers, it must have access to detail data as well as summary data.

Simple vs. Complex Queries

Why do you ask a question of your database? Not just to get an answer. You want an answer so you can create an action. It is actions, not answers, that have the daily impact on your business.

Queries, like any kind of question, can be simple or very complex. The following illustrates how different complexity levels in the queries can have dramatically different bottom line effects on your business.

> In this financial industry example, our customer is a bank. This bank offers a certain financial instrument which its competitor has decided to offer "free of charge." Obviously, the bank has to respond, or it will probably lose those customers who are currently paying an unnecessary fee for this financial instrument.

> In deciding how to respond, the bank might ask a simple question, like "Which of my customers are using our version of this product?" When the answer set is delivered, the bank would eliminate the annual fee for all of these customers. While this may help them

retain these customers, the overall result is that it has eroded the bank's profit.

But if the bank asked a complex query instead, the result will be quite different. By identifying the subset of its customers using this instrument that would still be profitable to the bank if the fee were eliminated, the bank can weed out its profitable customers and keep them, while giving the unprofitable ones to its competitor— who doesn't have a system that can tell him he's signing up unprofitable customers. This impact is entirely about profit maximization, and illustrates the value of a complex query over a simple query.

If we think back to the discussion we just had about how data is organized into tables, we can see that a simple query may only access one or two tables. This delivers a low-value answer, which enables a low-value action.

But a complex query is looking for all sorts of interrelationships. So a complex query will need to cover data across a great many tables, which as we said earlier makes for a processing and IO intensive environment. But this kind of question can deliver an answer that can enable very high-value actions.

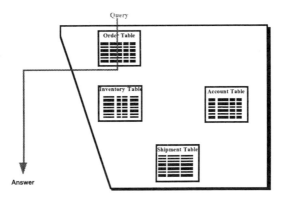

Figure 8: Simple Queries

The relationship between query complexity and the degree of detail of the data is also very clear. Simple queries can be asked of either summary data or detailed data. This is not true of complex queries.

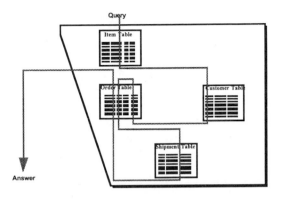

Figure 9: Complex Queries

A complex query often needs to access the lowest level of detail possible: hour of the day, purchase by customer name, every item in the customer's market basket. This means that complex queries cannot be asked of summary data. This is a very important relationship to understand, because if you decide you need to ask complex queries, you now know what that means about the degree of detail you will need in the data warehouse.

To summarize this section, complex queries deliver drastically greater business value than simple queries. But complex queries have two distinct dependencies:

1. They require access to multiple tables, which increases the processing complexity and raises issues regarding the database engine's ability to efficiently address these tables; and

2. They require detail data.

Ad-Hoc Queries

Humans are naturally inquisitive. Most learning and discovery occurs through a continuous process of asking questions, getting an answer, then asking another question based on the previous answer.

Increasingly, businesses are trying to become discovery-oriented. But for decades, information cultures have been based more on "reporting" than on "discovery."

In the traditional information culture of reporting, the business behaves in a reactive fashion. This is because in a reporting environment, all information is after-the-fact: a report is issued which describes what has already happened, so the business decision is to react to that event. Reporting-oriented information systems rely upon pre-defined questions, which dictate the dimensions of the report.

In a discovery-oriented environment, the questions are not known in advance. In this kind of an environment, the computer system must be able to handle the questions as they arise, or on an ad-hoc basis. When this approach is used, relationships are uncovered and the business can behave in a proactive fashion, making decisions to control future events instead of reacting to them after the fact.

This issue of discovery is an important point for data warehousing, since the trends fueling the data warehousing market are based on the need for information. Today's competitive environment is so fierce that companies need the best information possible to survive. Pre-defined reporting environments do not provide this kind of information. Increasingly, businesses are gravitating toward a discovery-based, ad-hoc information environment; and the system they choose to use must be able to support that kind of need.

There are two general drivers for ad-hoc queries. One is the situation where a person or group of people are responsible for digging through the enterprise data to find business opportunities. In the financial industry, such knowledge workers might be looking for cross-selling opportunities; in retail, they could be focused on market basket analysis; in communications, they might be looking for calling patterns that indicate a high risk of customer loss to a competitor; and so on.

The other situation is one where the business receives some kind of shock, and the business users want to find out why it happened. In the transportation industry, it may be an issue of over- or under-capacity; in communications, it might be an examination of sudden customer attrition.

In both of these situations, the user must have the freedom to ask questions as they arise, and the system must be able to accommodate this need. No business can know what questions it will need answers for tomorrow.

To summarize this section, it is essential to understand that an information culture based on discovery must be able to do ad hoc queries. And, in general, ad hoc queries will be complex. And, as we have seen in the previous section, complex queries require detail data. The real value in a data warehouse comes from being able to ask unplanned complex business questions on detail data. This is how you get the major returns on investment you expect from a data warehouse. Systems must be put into place that can achieve this goal. If the wrong systems are chosen, the value in the warehouse will be significantly reduced and may ultimately lead to failure instead of the expected business value.

The Dynamic Warehouse

Remembering our first key point— at the heart of a data warehouse is your data modeled to match your business. As the warehouse is used to change the business, so must the warehouse change to continue to reflect an accurate model of the business. In other words, a real production data warehouse sows the very seeds that require it to change. The only "static" warehouse, is the warehouse with little or no value to the business.

In addition to this inherent dynamic, detail data, complex queries and ad-hoc queries each place significant dynamic demands on the heart of the data warehouse. Ad-hoc implies unpredictable peak query loads. Queries will come from people with varying knowledge levels. And the number of people doing the ad-hoc analysis will vary unpredictably during each working day. Complex queries will scan a varying number of tables and analyze a varying amount of data, driving a varying level of IO and processor intensive work. The value in detail data will drive explosive growth in the number and size of the tables as well as the processing times needed to scan, retrieve, load and backup this data in ever shrinking batch windows.

The Data Warehouse is indeed a very dynamic environment. The number of sourcing systems will grow and change. On-line and batch updates will constantly change the data in the warehouse if it is to remain fresh. The number of data marts will grow and change. The number of applications, tools and users will grow and change. And the business the warehouse models will grow and change.

Conclusions

Since ad-hoc queries are frequently complex, there are issues of query complexity that call for a highly scaleable system. Detail data is required for complex queries. The industry has oversimplified the issue of scalability by referring to it as only an issue of data volume. While this is a critical issue by itself, it is only one of many issues that affect the performance of the overall system.

To support the IO and processor intensive workloads associated with Data Warehousing, the hardware platform must be scaleable in the amount of memory and number of CPUs and IO channels it can support in an SMP node and the number of SMP nodes it can support in an MPP environment. The database engine that runs on this platform must be able to scale the number of users, the number of tables, the number of rows in these tables, the number of summary tables and Data Marts, the number and type of data access tools, and the ever increasing demands on data loads from a growing number of source systems. It must also manage the varying daily workload mix associated with complex ad-hoc queries. In addition, it must keep all query workloads balanced over the entire SMP/MPP hardware configuration, scaling seamlessly as hardware is added. And it must do all of this in an automated fashion to prevent the number of administrative personnel from growing without bounds.

The true issue of scalability as it relates to the data warehouse is not just one of data volume. As we have discussed, every link in the data warehouse is dynamic. But unless the Heart of the Data Warehouse can accommodate all of the required dimensions of scalability, the entire data warehouse infrastructure will not be able to meet the complete needs of the business. Great care must be taken to insure that the hardware and software systems at the heart of the data warehouse are capable of sustaining the dynamic nature of the workload required to gain the maximum value from the warehouse.

Chapter 2

Paving the Way to Data Warehouse Project Success

—Doug Laney,
Consulting Manager
Prism Solutions, Inc.

Introduction

Data warehouse projects pose a truly unique set of analysis, design, technology and management challenges which are unlike traditional development projects. More than a set of technologies, successful data warehouse implementations are the result of an effective project approach. Confidently and effectively navigating your way through a data warehousing effort calls for a new kind of road map. This article addresses how traditional approaches can curb a data warehouse project while a data warehouse-specific road map will place a project in the fast-lane to success.

Architecture for the Ages

There are age-old data architectures, and architectures for old-aged data. In data warehousing we desire the latter. Even after reading the books and attending the seminars, without the experience it's hard to know exactly what to do. It's all too easy to fall back on what we've done before for the last 30 years. It's difficult to know how to, even if we do know we're supposed to:

- Create information models, not data models

- Design for analytical efficiency, not operational efficiency

- Introduce managed redundancy and denormalization, not shun them

- Tune the database for understanding and accessibility, not for update performance

- Embrace historical data, not overwrite it

- Be concerned more for temporal integrity than referential integrity

- Design to manage data content AND data context (meta data)

- Architect data delivery structures for multiple user communities, not a single one

The list of architectural differences goes on. By the time these architectural differences are noted (if they're noted at all), it's often too late for project managers to search for guidance. Probing traditional systems development life cycles (SDLC), business process re-engineering (BPR), or rapid application design (RAD) methodologies for answers is an exercise in futility. Regardless how many boxes or arrows or levels they may have, they're still geared toward developing operational systems which run the business, rather than informational systems to analyze and provide insight about the business.

Not only are the unique architectural considerations for data warehousing absent among common methodologies, but even worse: anything that looks remotely useful in one may in fact be the polar opposite of what an experi-enced data warehouse architect would advocate. Common methodologies and customary techniques, not technology, are largely to blame for data warehouse projects that are pulled over on the shoulder or have resulted in "fatalities."

The Data Warehouse Road Map

"Alright," you say, "we've put together an all-star data warehousing design team to hammer out these architectural issues— let's go!" Go where? Go when? With whom? How?

Successful data warehouse projects have process as a key consideration. Again, this is not a traditional development process, but one that accommodates the radical differences in expectations, involvement and activities between data warehouse endeavors and operational business system projects. Any successful data warehouse project needs a methodology, or road map, with three key features: iterative development, parallel scheduling, and data warehouse-specific work items.

Iterative Development

There is a practical reason and a political reason why successful data warehouse projects should be managed iteratively. First, data warehouses, by definition, bring together data from several operational (source) systems. Projects that attempt to bite off too many sources at one time are more likely to end up chasing their tails as one or more of the source systems undergoes maintenance or replacement.

Second, most data warehouses are built to allow the discovery of incredible new sources of business opportunity or glaring business inefficiencies. This creates expectations that are sky-high and introduces windows of opportunity for solving particular analytical problems. In addition, most data warehouses are built to allow the visibility and analysis of cross-functional data. All of this leads to wide-spread political frenzy, and brings about the need for exceptional levels of commitment and involvement.

A life cycle approach to developing data warehouses is contrary to the obvious differences in project pragmatics and politics. To effectively contain the politics and retain the commitment needed to deliver a successful data warehouse, it is imperative to manage scope by delivering iterative successes. Each data warehouse project iteration should have a limited scope focused on delivering a single analytical solution in a three-to-four month rigid "timebox." To this end, your data warehouse road map should illustrate the project on-ramps and off-ramps allowing you to reach many destinations along the way.

Parallel Scheduling

Consider the range of individual talents needed to deliver a data warehouse. You may need at least two distinct sets of technical talent— one for each of the source systems and one for the target (data warehouse) system. You will need at least five sets of tool vendors: computing platform, DBMS, extract-transformation, end user query/reporting tool, and meta data management. Each will be needed at different project phases. Include both designers and developers for the data access, data acquisition, and meta data management construction and you've only just begun. Consider business analysts, data warehouse architects, computer operations, networking, training development/delivery, marketing, and internal support— and now you've got a data warehouse development team!

Each of these sets of development personnel are needed at different points in the project and for different lengths of time. On successful data warehouse projects, sets of activities occur in concert, e.g. business requirements analysis, source systems analysis and data model analysis. However, project managers unfamiliar with building data warehouses often are inclined to take a conservative, serial "waterfall" approach to planning and scheduling for these distinct sets of talent. Unless parallel resource scheduling is done, even a well scoped iteration turns into a slow-paced 9 to 12 (or more) month effort.

Seasoned data warehouse project managers apply a parallel track approach to scheduling and managing talent to achieve the critical three-to-four month delivery timebox. It is customary for well managed projects to comprise up to five parallel process tracks including:

1. Project oriented activities focus on acclimating the company to data warehousing, aligning and managing the project team, implementing project training, establishing a support function, organizing internal marketing/communication, rolling out the data warehouse, and setting data warehouse strategic direction.

2. User oriented activities focus on understanding user data access/analysis requirements, modeling departmental data stores,

designing and constructing the end user access environment, providing user training, managing the user acceptance process and evaluating the data warehouse.

3. Data oriented activities focus on understanding existing operational data, modeling the atomic data warehouse structure, designing the data warehouse characteristics, creating the physical database, designing and constructing the data warehouse processing applications and populating and testing the data warehouse.

4. Technically oriented activities focus on understanding existing or possible data sources, sizing the data warehouse environment, and determining, configuring, setting up and testing the computing environment.

5. Meta data oriented activities focus on identifying existing sources of meta data, integrating technical and business meta data and designing/constructing a meta data delivery environment.

With parallel development, planning and execution as part of the road map, data warehouse projects will travel short streets of success rather than long freeways toward failure.

Data Warehouse-Specific Approach

As important as the differences in the project management process—iterative and parallel— the clear architectural differences between a data warehouse and operational system warrant a need for work items specific to data warehousing. As we have already discovered, traditional systems development methodologies at either end of the spectrum fly in the face of effective data warehouse project management techniques. On one end, traditional SDLC methodologies promote projects that are top heavy in analysis, and encourage addressing comprehensive sets of requirements over extended timeframes. On the other end, RAD methodologies promote the type of throw-away-and-do-it-again prototyping that is not conducive to projects that deal with the movement of gigabytes or terabytes of information.

Still, even if we were to tweak existing SDLC or RAD approaches to repair these shortcomings (as so many have attempted), major deficiencies, gaping holes, and erroneous techniques would remain. Aside from the fact that they would still not represent iterative or parallel processes, most of the techniques for architecting informational/analytical systems would be absent. The following are a few examples of the many activities missing from these concocted "SDLC-DW" or "RAD/DSS" methodology medleys:

- No source system analysis activities to establish the cleanliness, completeness, accessibility and availability of candidate "systems of record"

- No data model analysis focused on selected subject areas to determine the existence of data to meet analytical requirements

- No data mapping, transformation design, and integration flow design

- No multi-level data architecting for atomic and aggregated data structures

- No design of data cyclicity, volatility, and multiple-granularity, etc.

- No data warehouse development for extract processing, data transport, data loading, post-load processing, etc.

- No meta data analysis, collection, integration and delivery

Using a roadmap expressly designed for developing data will help you avoid the potholes and dead ends of either a traditional, or a patchwork approach.

Data Warehousing Best Practices

When contemplating data warehouse projects, managers too often fall into the trap of focusing on which technology to purchase and which skills to rent. True, a set of data warehouse "best tools" and "best talent" can be expensive. But the decision to forego a data warehouse "best practices" road map to guide the project is the costliest decision a project manager can make.

Methodology Consideration	Systems Development Life Cycle	Rapid Application Development	Data Warehousing Methodology
Business focus	Operational systems	Operational systems	Analytical systems
Management approach	Waterfall, conservative, discrete product	Prototyping/throw-away mentality	Iterative, parallel, builds on previous iterations
Analysis	Comprehensive, prolonged	Limited	Solution-focused source analysis, data analysis, business requirements analysis
Data modeling	Operational data	None/operational data	Atomic and departmental levels and design; meta data integration and delivery
Physical data design	Keys, indexing, partitioning	As needed	Multiple levels of data aggregation, history, volatility, cyclicity, and granularity; DBMS key structures, loading, indexing, and partitioning
Processing design	Operational processing	As needed	Data extract, transformation, integration, transport, loading, scheduling, monitoring
Testing	Operational processing	Operational processing	Data mobility processing and data validation
Evaluation	Meets acceptance criteria?	Meets business requirements?	Meets user requirements, management expectations, acceptance criteria? Iterative process improvement needed?
User involvement	Analysis and rollout	Frequent acceptance and redesign	Throughout
Scope maintenance	Sign-offs and checkpoints	Application redesign	Business problem focus, negotiated design, schedule timebox, parallel scheduling, iterative projects

Notes

Chapter 3

Selecting a Data Replicator

Evaluating Data Replication Alternatives

—Joel Klebanoff, Praxis Consultant

Introduction

*This paper assumes the reader both recognizes a business
opportunity for data sharing enterprise-wide and has decided to buy an
enterprise information sharing system rather than develop the
capabilities in-house. It addresses issues and product features you must
consider when evaluating data movement software.*

> *"The consumer, so it is said, is the king ... each is a voter who
> uses his money as votes to get things done that he wants done."*[1]

---

[1] Paul A. Samuelson, *Economics.* 8th edition, McGraw-Hill, Inc., 1970

As this white paper illustrates, there are several criteria to consider when evaluating data movement software. The relative ranking of the importance of each criterion varies among organizations.

View the following discussion in the context of your organization. When evaluating data movement software, assign importance weightings to the purchase criteria as best fits your needs.

For example, consider two enterprises: Company A spreads its data over DB2, Oracle and Informix databases, all on different hardware platforms. Company B enforces an immutable law that says there shall be a single platform throughout the organization. Heterogeneity— the ability to move data between diverse platforms— is a minimum requirement for Company A. Whereas, Company B, if it can adhere to its law, has little use for this feature.

Similarly, one possible data movement application is to enhance security by keeping the full database on a highly secure system and replicating non-confidential information to a less secure environment. Doing this requires partitioning— the ability to replicate or copy just portions of database tables. On the other hand, a company considering data movement software solely to maintain a backup of a complete database does not require partitioning.

Bear in mind more than just today's requirements. An enterprise information sharing system is the framework upon which data replication, copy management, and a wide variety of applications are built. The data movement software you buy today will likely serve your enterprise for many years. It must meet not just immediate needs, but also those of the future. Look at the overall architecture of the enterprise information sharing system to ensure it has the flexibility to adapt to changing requirements— some of which you do not even know today.

Fulfilling Needs

The process of selecting a data movement solution starts with your requirements. Most enterprises need the ability to share information within the corporation, between sites, and among different systems and applications. Before you can decide which data movement solution best suits your needs, you must first determine what those needs are— what and how do you want data to be distributed through the enterprise.

Applications

The first question is, of course, what the end result should be. The features needed to provide, for example, capacity relief for existing systems may be quite different from those needed to support the data requirements of a foreign subsidiary.

Environment

Another consideration is your computing environment. What hardware, operating systems and database management systems (DBMS) store the data now, and which will store it on the replicas? Obviously, the data movement solution you choose must support all of the necessary platforms, and be able to move data between them.

A solution capable of managing the flow of information between diverse hardware, operating systems and DBMSs in a single operation also opens new opportunities. While your data may now reside on a mainframe, the replica can use a lower cost UNIX system, thus increasing flexibility while decreasing cost.

Update Location

You also need to look at where you want data to be updated once it has been copied or replicated. Should users be able to update data at any site and have the updates reflected at all others, or is it acceptable to restrict updates to a single site? If you require the former capability, your choice of data movement solutions will be restricted. Some solutions do not offer an "update anywhere" capability. Instead, they may insist that you name one site as owner and sole authority for updating data.

The Need for Speed

Asynchronous replication (see *Synchronicity*, in this chapter), introduces a lag between when a user updates data on a local database and when the replicator applies the update to the remote replica(s).

For some applications, minimizing this lag is critical. In other cases, minutes, or even more, of delay are not an issue. In fact, some applications introduce intentional delays through a managed scheduling process.

Many organizations over-estimate the liability of data movement lags. Consider a clerk who keys data from forms that arrive by mail. Even without a data movement solution, the time before on-line users can access the data varies greatly depending on the speed of the postal service, the size of the stack of forms on the clerk's desk, and the clerk's keyboard skills. A small data movement lag has little effect on the end result.

Before evaluating a solution for enterprise information sharing you must determine how much of a lag is acceptable within the applications supported.

Meaning versus Form

32 = 0; 1 = 2.54; NY = New York; 12-4607 = pastel blue. All of these assertions are true under certain conditions. 32° Fahrenheit = 0° Celsius; 1 inch = 2.54 centimeters; NY is the abbreviation for New York; and, 12-4607 is the Pantone color code for pastel blue.

There are many other examples, such as product codes versus product descriptions, of equivalent meanings which take on different forms in different systems. Before considering a solution for enterprise information sharing, look at your applications and determine if these differences exist. If so, you must decide whether you will resolve and eliminate all differences before implementing the solution, or if the solution must support the differences and translate data as it flows between systems.

Enterprise Information Sharing

With an increase in managing numerous data stores, of which may exist in different databases and different systems, IS is faced with critical business challenges: How can this information be shared effectively? How does this information stay current, consistent, and synchronized? How does an enterprise manage this information?

Data replication, copy management, and data extracts and merges resolve some of these issues. However, to effectively manage all of these operations and ensure information consistency, an enterprise needs a unified information sharing model with a single control point that manages and monitors processes.

This model is the foundation for unifying data mapping, distribution routing, and synchronization scheduling for all data movement operations in an enterprise. The model, in essence, provides the glue between the diverse platforms in the organization. While data replication is the fundamental technology supporting the model.

An effective enterprise information sharing system supports multiple data movement methods and maintains consistency in the information selection operations and transformation rules.

Enterprise Information Sharing System Capabilities

The capabilities of an enterprise sharing system should be designed to enhance the features offered by data movement solutions. The design objective is to simplify the management of all operations and to simplify the processes by maintaining consistency throughout. Regardless of the data movement method used to distribute data, the enterprise sharing system monitors and tracks all processes and presents the information as a single view to the user.

A data replication solution that is incorporated into the framework of an enterprise information sharing system is relieved of the tedious tasks of re-registering data tables for each operation. The enterprise information system maintains a registration model allowing users to leverage existing registration information, without sacrificing flexibility. This registration model applies to all data movement functions.

Because the enterprise information sharing system maintains data models in its framework, synchronization between data tables is dynamically implemented at all nodes. When a new product, or a new version of an application is introduced into the distribution network, an enterprise information sharing system provides the same capabilities to dynamically update and synchronize the new application's data tables with the current tables in the model.

Data Replicator Features and Facilities

Replicator Architecture

The underlying architecture of the replicator affects its performance, and the features it can offer. The following sections describe some of these architectural differences.

Replication Administration and Control

A replicator must provide a means for you to define what data to replicate where. You must also be able to control replication, starting and stopping processes as required. In addition, the replicator should provide a means of monitoring the replication processes to allow for tuning of the architecture.

Whatever the vehicle provided for accomplishing these tasks, it should be easy and efficient to use, while giving you complete control over the process.

Change Capture

While this document assumes that a data replicator copies only changed data, that is not always the case. Some products which bill themselves as data replicators extract whole tables, or segments of tables, regardless of whether the data is changed during the replication cycle.

Benefits of Change Capture

- Eliminate batch copy windows thus opening opportunities for 7x24 applications.

- Reduce processing on the replica (fewer updates applied).

- Reduce network traffic (lower volume of data transferred).

Synchronicity

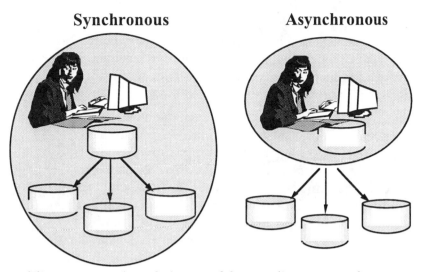

Synchronous   **Asynchronous**

There are two broad classes of data replicators: synchronous and asynchronous.

Synchronous replicators perform replication within the source update transaction, usually using two-phase commit. With synchronous replication the source transaction is not considered complete until the update has been applied to all replicas.

With an asynchronous replicator, the source update is independent of the replication process. The user's transaction completes when the local update is complete. The replicator updates the replicas only after the user transaction commits the changes to the local database. Replication may occur moments after the source transaction, in near real-time, or it may be scheduled for later execution.

As described in the *Log Versus Trigger-Based* section in this chapter, even using an asynchronous replicator, some of the processing may take place within the user transaction. The amount of work included within the scope of the user's transaction depends on the replicator.

The benefit of asynchronous replication is that it minimizes the impact on the user transaction and increases the robustness of the replication process. Users can continue with other work as soon as the local database applies the update, they do not have to wait for updates to be applied to the remote replicas.

This design also makes asynchronous replication more fault-tolerant. In the event of a network or replica failure, the replicator holds all updates in a persistent queue. The user continues working with the local database without regard to replication.

Synchronous replication has at least one advantage over asynchronous replicators. Since the local and remote updates are within the same unit of work, synchronous replication guarantees that all replicas will be identical at all times. With asynchronous replication, there will be some lag period, when the local and remote databases are inconsistent. This lag might be seconds for continuous replication, or longer for scheduled replication or in the event of system failure. For most applications, the momentary lag is far outweighed by the benefits of asynchronous replication.

The replication lag is also the reason why "data collisions" are possible when using bi-directional replication. The *Bi-Directional Capability* section in this chapter discusses this issue more fully.

Benefits of Asynchronous Replication

- With less processing attached to the user transaction, the user regains control of the system sooner.
- Users are not affected by network delays or slow remote processors.
- Users can continue work even in the event of network or remote database outages.

Benefits of Synchronous Replication

- All replicas remain fully synchronized at all times.
- The use of two-phase commit eliminates the possibility of data collisions.

Latency

As discussed above, asynchronous replication introduces a period of latency— the time after a user applies an update locally but before the replicator applies it to the replicas. The duration of this latency depends on the design of the replicator, and the workloads and speed of the network and the replication source and target systems. If your application demands near real-time synchronization of replicas, ask the vendor to provide an estimate of expected latency periods in your computing environment.

Log Versus Trigger-Based

An asynchronous replicator can be either log or trigger-based. A log-based replicator scans the logs maintained by the DBMS to find changes to data registered for replication. It then captures these changes, packages them in some way, and sends them to the replicas.

A trigger-based replicator executes code invoked by database triggers when a user changes data registered for replication. How much work the triggers do depends on the design of the replicator. In theory, a trigger-based replicator could be synchronous, with the trigger code assuming responsibility for updating the remote databases. However, since this approach eliminates the benefits of asynchronous replication, and makes heterogeneous replication difficult, replication triggers typically place changed data into a queue for processing by other modules.

Since log-based replication is fully asynchronous with users' transactions, there is a period of time after a user updates data before the replicator becomes aware of the update. This increases the complexity of collision detection for bi-directional replication (See *Bi-Directional Capability* in this chapter).

In addition, since there is a delay between the time the DBMS enters a transaction on the log and the time the replicator reads that transaction off the log, the replication latency period tends to be longer for log-based than trigger-based replicators.

Benefits of Log-Based Replication

- All "industrial strength" DBMSs maintain logs, but not all DBMSs provide triggers.
- None of the replication process is attached to the user transaction, hence the user regains control of the system sooner.

Benefits of Trigger-Based Replication

- Vendors usually guarantee upward compatibility of triggers as they introduce new versions, whereas most vendors consider logs to be internal components and do not promise to maintain their structure across versions. Hence, a new version of a DBMS likely will not require an upgrade of a trigger-based replicator but may require an upgrade of a log-based replicator.
- There is usually less lag between completion of the source transaction and updating of the replicas.
- It is usually easier to implement collision detection.

Fault-Tolerance

Replicator fault tolerance implies three conditions:

1. Users can continue to query data locally in the event of a network or remote system failure. However, if other nodes have update authority, the local database will not contain any data in remote replication queue(s) at the time of the failure, or any updates applied to a remote replica during the failure. The replicator resynchronizes all replicas after the failure is corrected.

2. Users of a replica enabled for updates (possibly all replicas when using bi-directional replication) can continue to update data locally in the event of network or remote replica failure. The replicator resynchronizes all replicas after the failure is corrected.

3. Replicator control, queue, and meta-data tables are recoverable in the event of a database failure at any replica supporting data updates.

The first condition is met by the definition of replication. Users access a local copy of the database which may be fed by a remote system, but is independent of it.

The second condition requires that the replicator maintain a persistent local queue of data changes regardless of whether it is connected to the network and the other replicas. The replicator should detect when the other replicas once again become available, and then resynchronize them by sending any data updates applied during the outage.

The final condition implies the availability of back-up and recovery procedures for the replicator's internal tables. This may be accomplished by a routine provided by the vendor, or by standard utilities if the tables are stored in a third-party DBMS.

Transaction Integrity

A single user transaction may update several rows from several data tables. All of these updates are part of a single unit of work (scope of commit) on the source system. Applying the updates in a different sequence on the replicas can result in referential integrity and other inter and intra-table consistency problems.

A replicator that maintains the order of updates within a transaction, and transmits all source transaction updates as a single unit of work on the replica is said to provide "transaction integrity" or "transaction consistency". Transaction integrity/consistency also implies that transactions will be applied to the target in the same order as on the source.

The alternative, a replicator that extracts changed data without regard to transaction consistency, may have updates rejected at the replica due to referential integrity enforcement. Further, where updates are interrelated, one change depending on the result of another, updates applied out of order may introduce inconsistencies between the replica databases.

Benefits of Transaction Consistency

- Avoid potential referential integrity errors.
- Maintain inter and intra-table consistency.

Registration: Push or Pull

Registration of data for replication can be either "push" or "pull." With a push architecture, an administrator at the source database specifies which data to replicate to which replicas. In a pull architecture, administrators or users at remote sites subscribe to the data they need.

Benefit of Push Registration

- Retain better control over the replication processes.

Benefits of Pull Replication

- Make it easier for users to get the data they need.
- Distribute the administration process, reducing the workload of a single administrator.

Application Independence

Application independence means, simply, that you do not have to change your applications to make replication work. This is accomplished by performing replication at a database level.

Benefits of Application Independence

- Minimize the work required to implement replication.
- Eliminate the possibility of creating database discrepancies due to inconsistent replication logic in different applications, or due to forgetting to code replication in one or more applications.
- Enable evolutionary migrations from one technology platform to another without modifying existing applications.

Routing Options

You must also consider whether the data replicator will easily and efficiently provide the replication routing you want to implement. There are three basic routing topologies, although your full replication schema may consist of a combination of these topologies linked together.

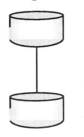

The simplest topology is a **single target**. In this case, a source database is linked to a single replica. This could be a uni-directional link with one replica acting as a read-only query, reporting or decision support database. Alternatively, it could be a bi-directional link allowing updating of data at either replica.

A **broadcast** topology is slightly more complex. Here, a single source replicates data to multiple targets. Most replicators are capable of broadcasting changes, but may differ in how 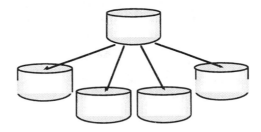 they do it. To minimize processing, particularly processing attached to the user's transaction, the replicator should capture changes once and then broadcast them to a distribution list. The alternative, capturing data changes multiple times, once for each target, significantly increases the required processing.

Another issue to consider is whether the target nodes in the broadcast topology can initiate changes. If so, what does the node at the center of the hub do with the change. Ideally, it should rebroadcast the change to the other targets, but not to the originating node.

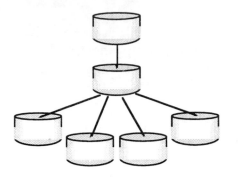

Cascade is an even more complex topology. In this scenario, a replica-tion target acts as a source for further replication.

Cascading replication can solve a problem faced by organizations that must replicate to a very large number of targets. While good replicator design captures changes just once regardless of the number of targets, it still must distribute the changes to all of them. The work involved in distribution is likely not an issue when there are just a few replicas. However, it could become a significant problem when the number grows.

Using a cascading topology, the enterprise can replicate changes to just one or a few distribution systems. These systems might be designated exclusively for the distribution task, or they may also support other applications. The intermediate distribution system(s) can then send data to the ultimate targets.

Questions to ask vendors about cascade capabilities include:

- Do changes have to be "recaptured" at the intermediate node or are they placed directly into a forwarding table? The former may increase the required processing.

- Can you partition data at the intermediate node? You may, for example, want to send all European data from Chicago to London, but forward from London to Paris only data for France, and forward from London to Munich only data for Germany.

- Can you enhance the data at the intermediate node? Each regional center may, for example, want to adjust prices to accommodate local market conditions before forwarding data to the stores in the region.

- Can this be bi-directional? And, if so, will all replicas remain synchronized regardless of where an update is applied?

Network Support

Yet another issue you must consider is support for the network protocol used by your organization. This is a straightforward question that can be answered by the vendors' sales literature or the vendors themselves.

Reconciling Database Differences

While, classified as "replicas," the source and target databases in a replication schema may not be exact duplicates. They may differ in database types, hardware platforms, naming conventions, partitioning of the data, and even the form of the data itself may differ. Many replicators offer a number of features to reconcile these differences automatically without the need to rewrite applications or convert the data in your existing databases.

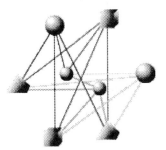

The following sections describe these features.

Heterogeneity

Heterogeneity is the ability to replicate between unlike platforms. The differences might be in the hardware (e.g., Sun SparcStation to IBM AS/400), operating system (e.g., MVS to UNIX), or database (e.g., DB2 to Informix).

In today's business environment, heterogeneity is often crucial. A survey of attendees at Gartner Group's Symposium 95 showed that fully 92% supported more than one DBMS in their organization. Of those, 58% supported 5 or more different database types and 28% supported 8 or more.[2]

There are many reasons for diverging DBMS platforms within a single enterprise:

- The organization adopts new technology platforms, yet, for economic or other reasons, legacy databases remain.

---

[2] *"The Realities of Enterprisewide DBMS Landscapes,"* research note, Gartner Group, December 28, 1995.

- The best available "off-the-shelf" application package does not run on the corporate standard DBMS, but the benefit of the package outweighs the cost of supporting another DBMS.

- Mergers and acquisitions force IT to support DBMSs used by the acquired and merged companies.

- Departments have autonomy over their systems, yet find they must share data.

Whatever the reasons, many organizations today face a DBMS Tower of Babel.

Even the 8% of organizations that now support only one DBMS will likely adopt new computing platforms in the future. Furthermore, some of these platforms are little more than a gleam in an engineer's eye today. When that time comes, because of the investment in existing systems, there will be some period when the enterprise must share data between old and new technologies.

Look at the underlying architecture of the data replicators under consideration to ensure they will meet your requirements. The first concern is support for existing computing platforms. Yet, more than that, the replicator must be sufficiently robust and flexible to adapt easily to the technologies of the future.

Benefits of Heterogeneous Support

- Collect data from diverse sources for query, reporting, and decision support.

- Transparently share data among disparate systems.

- Assist in the evolutionary migration from old to new technologies.

Data Type Conversion

DBMSs do not all share the same data types. A heterogeneous data replicator should be able to reconcile these differences, preferably automatically.

Even when both the replication source and target use the same DBMS, data types assigned to target columns may differ from those on the source. This might be a result of using replication to synchronize databases supporting two independently designed systems.

An organization may consciously choose different data types for a new replica when, for example, it realizes that the current precision of a column will not meet future needs. Without modifying the original database, it can create the new replica with the higher precision now, to avoid having to change it later. The organization changes the existing database only when required.

Benefits of Data Type Conversion

- Reconcile differences in data types supported by heterogeneous DBMSs.
- Support a phased migration to different data types.
- Meet the requirements of replicas supporting unique applications.
- Minimize recoding during application growth.

Source and Target Name Differences

Another question is support for different database, table and column names on the replication source and target.

Consider this scenario: Two legacy systems were developed independently, each with its own database. Because of the design of the systems, and the platforms used, they cannot share data, despite the existence of a large degree of redundant data. Currently, there are no links between the databases and users update each manually. As a result, users duplicate much of the data entry work. Furthermore, over time, the two databases developed many inconsistencies.

The company decided to spend considerable time and money to clean up the discrepancies. After doing so, it intends to enter the shared data into only one of the databases and use replication to copy the changes to the other.

However, while the data content is identical between the two systems, the table and column names are not. Changing the names would be a mammoth task since they are hard-coded in thousands of lines of application logic. In addition, users with access to the data through query and reporting tools have become familiar with the current names and would find it difficult to make the switch. Thus, the company decided that support for replication to tables and columns with different names was a critical criterion in its selection of a replicator.

Benefits of Support For Different Source and Target Naming

- Allow names that are more meaningful to local users.
- Support replication between databases using different naming standards.

Data Partitioning

Data partitioning is the ability to select only a portion of a database table for replication. A data replicator might provide one or both of two forms of partitioning:

Horizontal partitioning means replicating only particular rows. A further refinement is the ability to send different rows to different targets. So, for example, the head office database might contain the

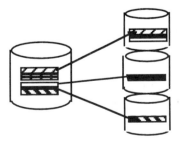

complete customer table, but a regional replica contains only rows with information about customers in that region. Taking this advantage to the extreme, you should be able to select any combination of rows for replication to any target, and possibly leave some rows unreplicated.

Vertical partitioning means replicating only particular columns. Again, a further refinement is the ability to send different columns to different targets. For example, a highly secure database table may contain confidential employee information, such as medical histories and salaries. A database table maintained specifically for the company infirmary might contain medical histories but not salary data. A table maintained for the accounting department might, instead, contain salary data but not medical histories. Vertical partitioning can replicate table columns on a need to know basis.

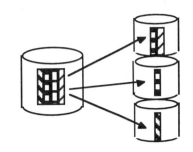

For maximum flexibility, a data replicator should offer a combination of vertical and horizontal positioning. With this capability, you can, for instance, replicate to the northeast region only the non-confidential columns of the employee table, and only rows pertaining to northeast region employees.

Benefits of Partitioning

- Reduce network traffic (transmit only data required by the replicas).
- Reduce replica system processing (updates only required data).
- Reduce replica disk requirements (contains only a subset of the source database).
- Improve security (replicate data on only a need-to-know basis).

Data Enhancement

While the word "replica" means "a copy," there are times when you want to copy the meaning, but not the precise form of data. Business analysts study the sales of "Vegetable Dicers," while the manufacturing group produces items with product code "A9386." What a United States paper company knows as "napkins," its Canadian subsidiary sells as "serviettes." Goods sold in pounds in the United States are sold in kilograms in Europe. The examples are endless.

A data replicator capable of data enhancement can transparently manage these variances. Each database stores its own local version of the data. The replicator reconciles the differences as it moves data from source to target.

Some questions to ask the vendor about data enhancement are:

- Do you offer it? Enhancement capabilities are far from universal.

- Is it integrated with the product? For convenience, you should be able to specify data enhancement requirements when you register data for replication.

- Will I have to do any programming to make it work?

- Can I extend the capabilities? A replicator offering data enhancement likely provides built-in routines. However, because of the broad range of unique needs, it is unlikely that built-in routines will meet 100% of your requirements. Check to be sure that you can easily expand the enhancement functions.

- Can I specify different enhancement routines for different replicas? While "red" is "rouge" in France, it is "rosso" in Italy.

- Can an enhancement create a single column out of many? For example, use "street address" plus "city" and "state" to find the appropriate zip code.

- Can an enhancement create multiple columns from one? For example, transform a "date" into "day," "month," and "year."

Applications of Data Enhancement

- Seamlessly manage local data variations.
- Translate codes into meaningful descriptions.
- Convert measurements (Fahrenheit to Celsius, inches to centimeters, etc.).
- Provide more useful information (for example, convert zip codes to regions for sales analysis).
- Support language differences in multilingual systems.

Benefits of Integrated Data Enhancement

- Save time programming transformations
- Save time managing new enhancements
- Save money testing and maintaining systems

Bi-Directional Capability

Bi-directional replication allows updating of data at any replica site. The replicator assumes responsibility for synchronizing the replicas.

Look closely at what a vendor means when they advertise bi-directional capabilities. Sometimes, when you ask what happens when two people update the same data at the same time, the answer is, "You have to design your databases so that can't happen." What they mean is that you must partition your database replicas so that each partition is owned, and can be updated by only one site.

This approach suffers two drawbacks. First, it might not meet your needs. You may want to implement replication specifically so that any data can be updated anywhere. Second, it is subject to errors. If the DBA makes a mistake setting up security you risk inconsistent data among replicas. The risk compounds when the original DBA moves on and a manager asks why she cannot update a certain set of data. The new DBA, not knowing the reason for the security scheme, may grant the manager update authority without taking it away from the site that owns it now.

True bi-directional replication provides "update-anywhere" capability for all replicated data. This, however, introduces the possibility of "data collisions"— two people updating the same data, at the same time, at different locations. To ensure data integrity, a bi-directional replicator must, at a minimum, offer collision detection and should also offer automated collision resolution.

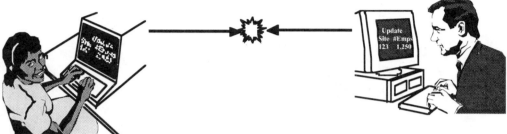

Collision Detection

How a replicator detects collisions varies depending on the replicator. It must, through some mechanism, determine if the data to be updated on the target is the same as that which was on the source before the user's transaction. If not, a collision occurred.

Collision Resolution

After detecting a data collision, the replicator must take some action. This might be as simple as logging the problem so an operator or the user can manually correct it. Alternatively, the replicator may automatically resolve the conflict based on a pre-determined algorithm.

The former approach, manual resolution, suffers obvious problems. It is subject to human error, it adds to workloads, and it increases the time when the two databases— no longer true replicas— remain unsynchronized.

Benefits of Bi-Directional Replication

- Reduce update response time through local processing at any replica.
- Keep most of the business operational in the event of a failure of the network or any one database node.

Special Features

The following sections describe special features which some replicators offer.

Scheduling Options

The replicator may offer a number of scheduling options:

Continuous replication captures changes as they happen and replicates them as soon as possible to the replica(s). This can result in near real-time replication.

Time of day scheduling specifies when replication will occur each day. For instance, replication may be scheduled for 2:00am to avoid times when systems and the network are otherwise busy.

Periodic scheduling specifies an interval between replication cycles. This may be a certain number of seconds, minutes, hours or days. Thus, replication could occur once a week, possibly on Sundays to avoid normal business hours.

Day of month scheduling specifies a day each month when replication will occur. This date is likely combined with a time of day. This can be useful for replicating to systems which must be attuned to business cycles. For example, to copy all of the previous month's financial data, replication can be scheduled to occur at 12:01 am on the first of each month.

Manual initiation allows an operator to decide when replication will occur. While this method requires operator intervention, and, hence, adds labor costs and the chance of human error, it may be preferable in some situations. If system processing and network loads are highly variable and unpredictable, an organization may have an operator monitor system conditions and initiate replication only during slow periods.

One must also consider what is being scheduled. With trigger-based replication, change capture is continuous regardless of scheduling of other replication processes. In this case, scheduling controls only the distribution of data to targets and any intermediate processes between change capture and data distribution. The design of the replicator determines system modularity and, hence, how many, if any, processes this includes.

If the replicator has a modular design it is preferable to be able to schedule all modules independently. This way, if you have only a narrow window for replication, you can minimize the work done within the window by scheduling intermediate processes to occur before data distribution, possibly even continuously. If, on the other hand, you have a long replication window, but strained resources during business hours, you can schedule all processes to occur during off-hours.

With a log-based replicator, it may also be possible to schedule the change capture portion of the replication processes— provided data updates applied since the last initiation of change capture are still available on the log at the scheduled time. This is likely not a problem if replication is frequent, but could become an issue for infrequent replication.

Benefits of Continuous Replication

- Maintain near real-time synchronization of replicas.
- Reduce the volume of replicated data traversing the network at one time.

Benefits of Scheduled Replication

- Shift replication processing and network traffic to off-hours.
- Synchronize replica databases on business cycle boundaries.

Netting of Changes

When replication is scheduled to occur periodically rather than continuously, some data items may be updated multiple times within the replication cycle. Some replicators can look at all updates to a data item and only send a single update reflecting the net effect. Other replicators send all updates. In the latter case, the target data item matches the source only after replication of all changes to it.

For some applications, net effect replication significantly reduces the volume of data sent and the amount of processing on the replica system. Without this netting capability, a system which, for instance, replicates month-end inventories from high-volume production lines might replicate several hundred updates, instead of one— the ending inventory level.

Netting of changes will be of little benefit when replicating updates continuously. In this case, the only time that changes accumulate on the source system is when there is a network or replica outage. There is, therefore, little chance to consolidate multiple updates to the same data.

Benefit of Netting Changes

- Reduce network traffic and replica system processing for high volume update databases when using low frequency scheduled replication.

Supporting Software

A cartoon which circulated around the information technology (then called data processing) community several years ago showed a complex flow chart. The chart contained hundreds of small rectangles, ovals, diamonds, circles, and some indescribable polygons. Each shape had at least one, and often more, lines going into it, and still more coming out. At the bottom of this long flow chart were the words, "And then a miracle happens."

Examine the architecture of each replicator under evaluation to be sure there are no places which say, or imply, "And then a miracle happens." Sometimes, to complete the picture you must buy, often complex and expensive, additional software to make the replication solution work. This might mean the acquisition of a gateway or other middleware product.

Be sure to determine these requirements before you complete your evaluation of the alternatives. The need for additional software could have a significant impact on the complexity and cost of the complete solution.

Coding Requirements

"With just a few lines of code" is likely the most abused phrase in the information technology industry. Like the need for additional software pieces, a vendor may promise certain features, such as heterogeneity or data enhancement, but when questioned, the answer comes back, "Well, it does take a few lines of code." When you go to write those few lines, you may find that your definition of "a few" varies considerably from the vendor's definition.

Before evaluating replicators, first develop a clear picture of your current needs, and some forecast of future requirements. Take those requirements to the vendors and have them show you how their product will fulfill the need, and what, if any, additional coding will be required.

Cost

Once they understand your requirements, data replicator vendors will readily quote you the price of their software needed to fulfill them. Since this price can vary over time, and depends on the number and type of replication nodes, this paper cannot give precise pricing.

When comparing prices of data replicators it is important to look at the total solution cost. Review the "*Supporting Software*" and "*Coding Requirements*" sections above. As these sections suggest, depending on which features you need, some vendors may require that you buy additional software components, purchase consulting services, or code them yourself, to achieve the desired outcomes. The comparable costs are, then, the **total** of the cost of all software, as well as the development costs for any components you must code yourself or outsource.

There are other costs that may differ among the various replication alternatives. The ease of use and implementation of a replicator affects the cost to prepare the software for operation and to train your people in its use.

Thus, to compare the costs of the various alternatives you must consider:

- The cost of the data replication software.

- The cost of a data distribution management tool.

- The cost of additional software, if any, such as gateways.

- Internal development costs, if any, required to implement the solution.

- Training costs.

- Implementation costs.

Notes

Chapter 3, Addendum

Features Checklist

Evaluating Data Replication Alternatives

—Joel Klebanoff, Praxis Consultant

This chart is printed with the permission of Praxis International, Inc.
Copyright © 1996, 1997 by Praxis International, Inc.

OmniReplicator is a trademark of Praxis International, Inc. All other trademarks and trade names are used to identify entities claiming the marks of their products.

Introduction

The following checklist list shows features recommended in a replication product.

Feature	Product		
Heterogeneity - Sources			
Heterogeneity - Targets			
Data type conversion			
Accept different source & target naming standards			
Bi-directional capabilities			
Conflict detection			
Conflict resolution			
Change capture			
Horizontal partitioning			
Vertical partitioning			
Data enhancement			
Synchronicity			
Latency			
Log or trigger-based			
Fault-tolerance			
Routing Options			
Scheduling options			
Transaction integrity			
Application independence			

Feature	Product		
Netting of changes			
Push or Pull			
Mobile computing support			
Replication administration			
Supporting software requirements			
Coding requirements			

Notes

Chapter 4

Building Decision Support Systems for Quick ROI

—PLATINUM *technology, inc.*

Introduction: Define the Project Scope

The key to success is like the old campaign slogan "keep it simple stupid."
Focus the project by business unit or department, prioritize deliverables, and
plan for constant and incremental deliverables.

Focus the Project by Department or Business Unit

For quick ROI, you need to have a focused effort and specific deliverables. Don't try to solve the entire company's problems with a single application. Find a logical way to divide decision support systems (DSS), such as by business units or by departments. Each department has specific business needs, decisions that need to be made to help it meet its goals. Those goals may be to decrease costs, increase quality ratings, decrease customer calls, increase profits. The following benefits can be derived by confining a decision support system and its underlying data warehouse to a single business unit:

- Key goals will be easier to identify and prioritize, thus making the objectives of the decision support system easier to define

- Fewer decision makers mean faster decisions when designing the system

- Because the project is initiated by the business unit decision makers, rather than a corporate it group, management buy-in is immediate and explicit

- Source data may be derived from fewer sources, making the data collection, transformation, and movement process easier

- Fewer business models and data definitions will need to be agreed upon to get the system up and running, decreasing design time

- Smaller data warehouses or data marts may mean that smaller purchases in hardware, software, and consulting can allow the data mart project to be completed within the business unit, using corporate IT as an advisor rather than as project implementor

Prioritize Deliverables

Don't Design the Perfect System and Wait for Its Delivery. One of the biggest mistakes that companies make is spending a tremendous amount of time up front designing a perfect world that is too costly and complex to execute before business priorities shift and the project is canceled. This is particularly true when enterprise-wide systems are designed to be all things to all people. Successful decision support systems are designed with limited but expandable scope to ensure that value is constantly delivered. This approach ensures immediate usefulness of the system and future funding.

Prioritize the Knowledge Needed First for Business Decisions.
Another key factor in success is determining *what* knowledge is needed and
when it's needed. Key decision makers have to make tough prioritization
decisions. This means not only putting items at the top of the queue, but
also putting items at the bottom of the queue and sometimes eliminating
items altogether.

Staged Deliverables

It's important to plan for constant, incremental deliverables. Deliverables
should be scheduled and delivered every quarter, reflect business priorities,
and accurately represent the development cycle.

Scheduled Deliverables. Every quarter the business unit owning the
DSS should see a deliverable and a specific ROI attached to that deliverable.
This effort keeps the development team focused and provides justification of
the project on an ongoing basis. The key to success is seeing constant, if
smaller ROIs, that will grow into the larger, long term ROI.

Business Priorities. System deliverables should always reflect business
priorities and should be re-evaluated every quarter for the four quarters to
come. This will ensure that the system adapts to changing needs while
providing timely, meaningful benefits.

Development Cycle. While it may seem ideal to have a system delivery
timetable that exactly mirrors the business priorities, accurate development
estimates may change the priority of some deliverables. For example, the
number one business problem may be solved with the most complex
technical solution that takes thirty person-months to deliver. If a secondary
business problem can be solved very quickly and with little effort, it may
deserve higher priority.

An organization should carefully select the appropriate balance between
technical resources and business priorities. Organizations often get lost in
the "ideal" warehouse and don't take advantage of quick deliverables that can
provide immediate ROI, even if they are not the main project deliverable.

Changing Requirements

As users begin to use the system to make business decisions, the way they
do business and the way they make decisions will change. Their original
expectations may not match their new business processes. Encourage this
new type of thinking, but manage change expectations over the long term,

not the short term. This approach allows a focused effort to deliver immediate payoff on the current implementation while accommodating new requirements in future phases.

Key Players

By limiting the scope of the project to a department or business unit, you can ensure that all key players are actively involved on an ongoing basis and that the system meets their needs. This means involving them in the quarterly reviews. And, with fewer people involved, decisions are made quickly so active business user involvement becomes an advantage, not a disadvantage.

Understand the Business Model

Why the Project Manager Must Understand Your Business

The data warehouse or decision support project manager is not simply a development project manager (although that aspect of the job certainly cannot be ignored). He or she must understand your business and your particular organization, including its partners and its competitors. The project manager should be able to guide key decision makers not only in the technical design of the warehouse, but also in selecting which parts of the application to roll out first. This advice should be based on experience with similar projects.

Internal vs. External

Project managers can come from within your organization or from outside firms that specialize in data warehousing. There are advantages and disadvantages to each route.

Internal: Knowing your Organization. One advantage of using an internal project manager is that an inside person will understand your organization, the key players, and the existing data stores and applications.

On the other hand, compared to an external project manager, an inside person may not have knowledge of how other companies have solved similar problems or extensive knowledge of new technologies. In addition, it's often difficult to keep internal project managers focused as they struggle to balance the project with other responsibilities.

External: Leveraging Industry Knowledge. There are several advantages of using an external project manager if you choose the right consulting company. In addition to having broader knowledge of similar projects and available technologies, outside consultants are somehow always more convincing to upper management than internal technical staff.

If you consider using an outside project manager, make sure they use an experienced-based methodology. It's also important that they have experience with decision support systems that are similar to yours, preferably in your industry. They should also have an understanding of other industries' data models that could potentially be adapted for use in creating your data model. And finally, they should have broad knowledge of leading technologies.

If you choose an external project manager, be certain to identify an internal liaison who will have responsibility for helping the consultant navigate the organization.

Build the Data Mart

Understand the Sources

Your Organization's Data. A thorough understanding of your organization's data is essential to build an effective data mart. You will need to identify where the data is located, what format it is in, how reliable or accurate it is, and how it will be used in business decisions.

Data Technology. It's important to have experience and knowledge in all database technologies in order to thoroughly evaluate the advantages and disadvantages of each. When researching database technologies, you should consider other successes within your organization; this will make procurement and installation and future integration easier. If you will be selecting a new DBMS, be sure to evaluate cost of ownership and maintenance; processing speed at small, medium, and large volumes; integration with existing technology; and industry leadership.

Define the Targets

Industry-Specific Data Models. Vertical warehouse application products are available to serve industry-specific needs, such as a decision support data mart designed to service the insurance industry. Part of the value of such a product is that it includes data models that reflect the kind of business decisions the specific industry needs to consider. If a vertical warehouse application is not available for your industry, you should consider engaging a data warehousing consulting company that can bring knowledge of your industry to your organization. Understanding of industry trends adds value and reduces implementation time, because the data models specific to your organization are built on a well-defined template. However, all companies have individual needs, so be sure that the solution you select is flexible enough to meet your future needs.

Design with Performance in Mind. When designing the data mart, design it with performance in mind. Do as much data manipulation (summaries, averages, etc.) before the data movement stage and outside the DBMS engine. This reduces the load on the processing machine and also reduces network traffic as the data mart is used more frequently by more users.

Transform and Move the Data

In the transformation process, the data administrator defines the sources and targets, including any unions, joins, or manipulation. Including the data manipulation in the transformation process, rather than within the DBMS engine, not only improves performance, it ensures data consistency by removing the definitions from the end users and giving it to data administrators. For mapping and performing transformations, organizations can choose either programming or using software tools. There are cases in which both methods are appropriate, but a data transformation tool provides a number of benefits, including ensuring that transformations are documented and stored in a repository so that they can be shared throughout the enterprise. When selecting a transformation tool, organizations should also make sure that it provides an automated and reliable method to move and update the data.

Keeping the Data Fresh

Understanding the objectives of the application ensures that the data is refreshed only as often as the business need requires. For example, daily inventory management requires daily change propagation, while trend analysis does not require frequent updates. Once you've determined how frequently data needs to be updated, consider how much data is affected. If more than 20% of the data is going to be updated, you may find it more efficient to do a complete refresh.

Your update strategy should be considered when evaluating transformation and movement tools to make sure they can support your data update requirements. You may also want to consider evaluating third party database utilities, such as PLATINUM Fast Load, to load the data more quickly, rather than loading through the DBMS engine.

Designing a Flexible End User System
Business Intelligence

When designing a data mart, selecting a flexible user interface is key to meeting end-user needs. A variety of business intelligence tools are available, for on-line analytical processing (OLAP), for quick deployment of graphical enterprise information system (EIS) applications, or for enterprise-class reporting. Selection of a user interface must not only address current needs, but also future needs. It must be flexible enough to accommodate changing user needs, but should also provide for future growth.

Experienced Project Management
Methodology

Experienced-based methodology provides an organization with the wisdom of those who have gone before. It ensures that a standard procedure is successful and repeatable. A data mart implementation without a proven methodology behind it is unlikely to be delivered on time or within budget.

Process Management

Strong process management should be a part of the data warehouse methodology and will be a key factor in the project's success. To further strengthen process management, organizations may want to consider implementing a project and process management software solution.

Repository

Repositories provide management services not only for data definitions, but also for systems management, application packages, and technology components. Thus, a repository implementation can manage process management information as well as data transformation information.

Change and Configuration Management

A data mart that will be continually enhanced needs application management to ensure that changes to the code are implemented, tested, and rolled out correctly. For most organizations, this means extending the processes and products already used for change and configuration management. Organizations that have not yet implemented change and configuration management software may want to consider products for mainframe management or for open systems.

Planning for Growth and Integration

The focus of this paper is how to get quick return on your decision support investment. However, any data warehouse, data mart, or decision support system design should plan for growth and integration into other systems within the company, including an enterprise-wide data mart. Tempting as it is to build a system that meets your needs only, if you want to make sure your investment is a long term one and that your system is not junked for the new corporate system, you need to consider using consistent data definitions and incorporating an ongoing maintenance plan.

Consistent Data Definitions

When defining data models for your system, select those data definitions that you know go beyond your business unit. These are definitions that would make sense to roll-up into a corporate data warehouse or to integrate with another department's system. For example, "product revenue" is something that most companies would want a common definition of so that company-wide analysis is possible. Other key terms may include "customer," "profit," "ship-date," etc. Work with a corporate group to ensure that you have defined these terms appropriately for the business. Once you've ensured that the data definitions are consistent, you can manage those definitions using a key reference table or a full repository implementation.

Key Reference Table Implementation. When implementing a departmental data mart, many organizations may not want to consider a full repository implementation as part of the core project. However, organizations can gain many of the benefits of a repository implementation, particularly those related to data consistency, by implementing a portion of the repository solution. This would include:

- Scanning only applications that will be used as sources for the data mart and storing that meta data,

- Using an end user access tool to understand meta data in business terms,

- Storing target definitions in the repository for repeatability (access by other applications and departments) and reusability for fast new application development, and

- Storing key data definitions for multi-department data consistency in the repository.

This approach provides the benefits of shareable information about data, data consistency throughout the enterprise, and provides an excellent head start toward a full repository implementation.

Full Repository Implementation. As part of the initial data mart implementation or as an add-on, organizations may choose to implement a repository. A full repository implementation can provide the data consistency benefits described above for the data mart as well as other critical applications and for the systems and applications management benefits described earlier. Repositories must support the languages and CASE tools used by your organization and should store meta data in relational database such as DB2, Oracle, Sybase, or Informix, rather than a proprietary data store.

Ongoing Decision Support System Maintenance

System Like All Others. The data mart application is a system like every other and it needs to be managed and maintained over time. When designing a solution, keep in mind the long term management issues. When evaluating tools, you should look for a vendor that understands data marts and can provide a complete solution.

Traditional areas such as performance management and tuning, database administration, and security are not essentially different than those in OLTP systems. However, there are areas like backup and recovery that may require a different approach. For example, depending on the size of the data mart, you may choose not to do a backup, because you can refresh the data mart more efficiently— just as if it were the weekly refresh.

Integrated, Easy to Maintain Solution

Choosing the right data warehousing vendor can be crucial to the success of your data mart. It's important to choose a vendor who:

- Understands the business and technology issues,

- Provides an experienced-based methodology,

- Provides data transformation and movement solutions,

- Provides data consistency through repository technology,

- Provides ongoing systems and database management solutions, and

- Has a consulting force that can provide senior level project managers as well as education, training, and implementation consultants for end-to-end solution.

Chapter 5

The Case for Relational OLAP

—MicroStrategy, Inc.

Executive Summary

IT organizations are faced with the challenge of delivering systems that allow knowledge workers to make strategic and tactical decisions based on corporate information. These decision support systems are referred to as On-Line Analytical Processing (OLAP) systems, and they allow knowledge workers to intuitively, quickly, and flexibly manipulate operational data using familiar business terms, in order to provide analytical insight. In general, these OLAP systems need to (1) support the complex analysis requirements of decision-makers, (2) analyze the data from a number of different perspectives (business dimensions), and (3) support complex analyses against large input (atomic-level) data sets.

There are two prominent architectures for OLAP systems: multidimensional OLAP (MD-OLAP) and relational OLAP (ROLAP). MD-OLAP architectures utilize a multidimensional database to provide analyses; their main premise is that OLAP is best implemented by storing data multidimensionally. In contrast, ROLAP architectures access data directly from data warehouses; ROLAP architects believe that OLAP capabilities are best provided directly against the relational database. When comparing these two architectures, the following observations can be made:

- *ROLAP leaves the design trade-off between query response time and batch processing requirements to the system designer, as the ROLAP architecture is neutral to the amount of aggregation in the database. MD-OLAP generally requires most of the database to be precompiled in order to provide acceptable query performance, thereby increasing batch processing requirements.*

- *Systems with high data volatility, namely those with changing data aggregation rules and user-defined consolidations, require an architecture that can dynamically consolidate data for ad hoc and decision support analyses. ROLAP is very well suited for dynamic consolidations whereas MD-OLAP is biased towards batch consolidations.*

- *ROLAP can scale to a large number of business analysis perspectives (dimensions), while MD-OLAP generally performs efficiently with ten or fewer dimensions.*

- *ROLAP supports OLAP analyses against large volumes of input (atomic-level) data. In contrast, MD-OLAP provides adequate performance only when the input data set is small (fewer than five gigabytes).*

Conclusion: ROLAP is a flexible, general architecture that scales to meet the widest variety of DSS and OLAP needs. MD-OLAP is a particular solution that is suitable for departmental systems with small data volumes and limited dimensionality.

Background

The ability to act quickly and decisively in today's increasingly competitive marketplace is critical to the success of organizations. The volume of information that is available to corporations is rapidly increasing and frequently overwhelming. Those organizations that will effectively and efficiently manage these tremendous volumes of data, and use the information to make business decisions, will realize a significant competitive advantage in the marketplace.

Advent of Data Warehousing

Data warehousing, the creation of an enterprise-wide data store, is the first step towards managing these volumes of data. The data warehouse is becoming an integral part of many information delivery systems because it provides a single, central location where a reconciled version of data extracted from a wide variety of operational systems is stored. Over the last few years, improvements in price, performance, scalability, and robustness of open computing systems have made data warehousing a central component of IT strategies. As Figure 1 illustrates, the data warehousing marketplace is expected to increase to a $7 billion industry with a 35% compound annual growth rate by 1999.

Figure 1: Data Warehouse Market Segment Revenue Forecast

	1994	1999	Compound Annual Growth Rate (CAGR)
Total Market Size	**$1,568.0**	**$6,960.0**	**34.7%**
Data Extraction/Movement	$65.0	$210.0	26.4%
Administration	$10.0	$450.0	114.1%
RDBMS	$288.0	$1,100.0	30.7%
Hardware	$1,075.0	$3,950.0	29.7%
Consulting Services	$130.0	$1,250.0	57.3%

All revenues are in millions of U.S. dollars and are Gartner Group estimates. Source: Gartner Group, Inc.

Not only is the size of the industry increasing at a very rapid rate, the quantities of information that organizations wish to access for decision-making purposes are also increasing.

Figure 2 shows that more than 70% of the organizations surveyed plan to implement data warehouses that are greater than 50 gigabytes in size, and more than 50% are planning data warehouses of over 100 gigabytes.

Figure 2: Growth in Data Warehouse Size

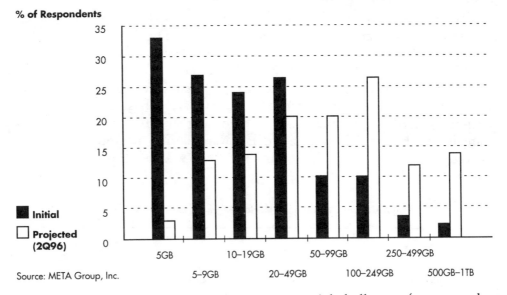

Source: META Group, Inc.

Building a data warehouse has its own special challenges (common data model, common business dictionary, etc.) and is a complex endeavor. However, just having a data warehouse does not provide organizations with the often-heralded business benefits of data warehousing. To complete the supply chain from transactional system to decision maker, IT organizations need to deliver systems that allow knowledge workers to make strategic and tactical decisions based on the information stored in these data warehouses. These decision support systems are referred to as On-Line Analytical Processing (OLAP) systems, and are discussed in the following section.

Requirements for OLAP

OLAP systems allow knowledge workers to intuitively, quickly, and flexibly manipulate operational data using familiar business terms, in order to provide analytical insight. For example, by using an OLAP system, decision makers can "slice and dice" information along a customer dimension and view business metrics by product and through time. Reports can be defined from multiple perspectives that provide a high-level or detailed view of the performance of any aspect of the business. Decision makers can navigate throughout their database by drilling down on a report to view elements at finer levels of detail or by pivoting to view reports from different perspectives. To enable such full-functioned business analyses, OLAP systems need to (1) support sophisticated analyses, (2) scale to large numbers of dimensions, and (3) support analyses against large atomic data sets. The following sections explore these three key requirements.

OLAP systems need to support sophisticated analyses

Decision makers use key performance metrics to evaluate the operations within their domain, and OLAP systems need to be capable of delivering these metrics in a user-customizable format. These metrics may be obtained from the transactional databases, may be precalculated and stored in the database, or may be generated on demand during the query process. Commonly used metrics include:

- Multidimensional Ratios (Percent to Total)
  Show me the contribution to weekly sales and category profit made by all items sold in the Northeast stores between May 1 and May 7.

- Comparisons (Actual vs. Plan, This Period vs. Last Period)
  Show me the sales to plan percentage variation for this year and compare it to that of the previous year to identify planning discrepancies.

- Ranking and Statistical Profiles (Top N/Bottom N, 80/20, Quartiles)
  Show me sales, profit and average call volume per day for my 10 most profitable salespeople, who are in the top 10% of worldwide sales.

- Custom Consolidations (Financial Consolidations, Market Segments, Ad Hoc Groups)
  Show me an abbreviated income statement by quarter for the last four quarters for my Central Region operations.

OLAP systems need to be dimensionally scaleable

Knowledge workers analyze data from a number of different perspectives or dimensions. For the purposes of this paper, a dimension is any element or hierarchical combination of elements that can be displayed orthogonally to other combinations of elements in the data model. Taking a particular scenario, if a report lists sales by week, promotion, store, and department, it would be a four-dimensional slice of data— see Figure 3.

**Figure 3: OLAP Report
with Four Dimensions**

		Promotion 1		Promotion 2	
		Store A	Store B	Store A	Store B
	Dept A	667	592	221	407
Week 1	Dept B	877	362	718	543
	Dept C	415	445	236	745
	Dept A	902	534	307	425
Week 2	Dept B	653	716	431	298
	Dept C	609	366	250	514

Target marketing and market segmentation applications involve extracting highly qualified result sets from large volumes of data. For example, a direct marketing organization might want to generate a targeted mailing list based on dozens of characteristics, including purchase frequency, purchase recency, size of the last purchase, past buying trends, customer location, age of customer, and sex of customer. These applications rapidly increase the dimensionality requirements for analysis.

The number of dimensions in OLAP systems range from a few dimensions to hundreds of dimensions. Figure 4 contains sample orthogonal dimensions for Retail, Banking, and Utility OLAP applications.

OLAP systems need to support large atomic data sets

Atomic data refers to the lowest level of data granularity required for effective decision making. In the case of a retail merchandising manager, atomic may refer to information by store by day by item. For a banker, it may be information by account by transaction by branch. Most organizations implementing OLAP systems find themselves needing systems that can scale to tens, hundreds, and even thousands of gigabytes of atomic information. (Refer to sidebar for specific examples, *Organizations Collect Large Volumes of Atomic Data*.)

As OLAP systems become more pervasive and are used by the majority of the enterprise, more data over longer time frames will be included in the data store, and the size of the database will increase by at least an order of magnitude. OLAP systems need the horsepower to be able to scale from present to near-future volumes of data.

Figure 4: Sample Orthogonal Dimensions

Retail	Banking	Utility
• region–market–state–store	• account type–account bank–	• division–department–
• department–class–item	household–segment	response center–cost center–
• color–item	• household–zip	subproject–work order–
• size–item	• year–quarter–month–week–day	work instruction–operation
• year–month–day	• activity type	• team–work instruction–operation
• week–day	• household–major market	• group–category–finance code
• promotion period–day	• fiscal year–fiscal quarter–	• expense category–subproject–
• demography–store	fiscal month–week	work order–work instruction–
• manager–sales rep–store	• region–state–bank–branch	operation
• state–customer	• account bank–branch–account #	• level A activity–level B activity–
• age–customer		level C activity–level D activity–
• gender–customer		activity
• style–item		• project–subproject–work order–
• distribution center–store		work instruction–operation
• vendor–item		• cost year–cost month–cost week
		• manager–work order–
		work instruction–operation

Organizations Collect Large Volumes of Atomic Data

A retail business with 200 stores and 350,000 products (of which an average of 100,000 are sold in any given store) that records just revenue information for 13 months at the daily level would have atomic data of approximately 160 gigabytes of information (assuming 20 bytes per row). When inventory, planned sales, promotional, supplier, demo-graphic, and seasonal information are included in the system, this number can rapidly exceed 500 gigabytes.

A banking DSS for evaluating household profitability might have 300,000 accounts, 18 months of daily data, 300 branches, and 40 possible activities. There is some degree of sparsity in this model (i.e., each account does not execute every transaction at every branch on every day). Assuming that just four out of every thousand possible transaction combinations takes place, simply storing the level of funds involved in each transaction requires approximately 90 gigabytes of atomic data. This is certainly a low-end calculation when the multitude of other information typically required by banking systems is taken into consideration. Customer information is essential for targeting and evaluating the various products of the bank.

Customer segment, market, zip code, related accounts, interest rate, credit ranking, number of times past 30 days due, and loan status are all examples of useful characteristics that a bank might require in its DSS. Incorporating these characteristic dimensions into the data model can dramatically increase the size of the system. It is quite common for a banking DSS such as this one to have well over 750 gigabytes of atomic-level information.

Two Architectures for On-Line Analytical Processing

Vendors of OLAP products are classified as either multidimensional OLAP or relational OLAP based on the underlying architecture of the system. This section describes some of the key components of each architecture.

Multidimensional OLAP: Architecture Overview

Multidimensional OLAP (MD-OLAP) utilizes a proprietary multidimensional database (MDDB) to provide OLAP analyses. *The main premise of this architecture is that data must be stored multidimensionally to be viewed multidimensionally.*

Figure 5 outlines the general MD-OLAP architecture. Information from a variety of operational systems is loaded into a multidimensional database through a series of batch routines. Once this atomic data has been loaded into the MDDB, the general approach is to perform a series of calculations in batch to aggregate along the orthogonal dimensions and fill the MDDB array structures. For example, revenue figures for all of the stores in a state would be added together to fill the state level cells in the database. After the array structure in the database has been filled, indices are created and hashing algorithms are used to improve query access times.

Figure 5: Multidimensional OLAP (MD-OLAP) Architecture

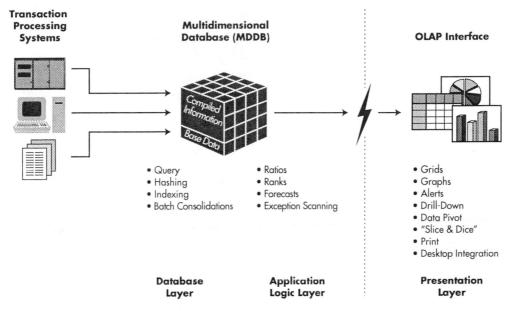

Database Layer	Application Logic Layer		Presentation Layer

Once this compilation process has been completed, the MDDB is ready for use. Users request OLAP reports through the interface, and the application logic layer of the MDDB retrieves the stored data. The MD-OLAP architecture is a compilation-intensive architecture. It principally reads the precompiled data, and has limited capabilities to dynamically create aggregations or to calculate business metrics that have not been precalculated and stored.

MD-OLAP is a two-tier, client/server architecture. In this architecture, the MDDB serves as both the database layer and the application logic layer. In the database layer, the MDDB system is responsible for all data storage, access, and retrieval processes. In the application logic layer, the MDDB is responsible for the execution of all OLAP requests. The presentation layer integrates with the application logic layer and provides an interface through which the end users view and request OLAP analyses. The client/server architecture allows multiple users to access the same multidimensional database.

Relational OLAP: Architecture Overview

Relational OLAP (ROLAP) accesses data stored in a data warehouse to provide OLAP analyses. *The premise of ROLAP is that OLAP capabilities are best provided directly against the relational database, i.e., the data warehouse.* An overview of this architecture is provided in Figure 6.

Figure 6: Relational OLAP (ROLAP) Architecture

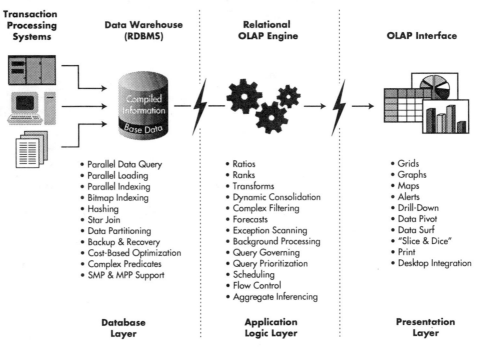

Transaction Processing Systems	Data Warehouse (RDBMS)	Relational OLAP Engine	OLAP Interface
	• Parallel Data Query • Parallel Loading • Parallel Indexing • Bitmap Indexing • Hashing • Star Join • Data Partitioning • Backup & Recovery • Cost-Based Optimization • Complex Predicates • SMP & MPP Support	• Ratios • Ranks • Transforms • Dynamic Consolidation • Complex Filtering • Forecasts • Exception Scanning • Background Processing • Query Governing • Query Prioritization • Scheduling • Flow Control • Aggregate Inferencing	• Grids • Graphs • Maps • Alerts • Drill-Down • Data Pivot • Data Surf • "Slice & Dice" • Print • Desktop Integration
	Database Layer	**Application Logic Layer**	**Presentation Layer**

After the data model for the data warehouse is defined, data from transaction-processing systems is loaded into the database. Database routines are run to aggregate the data, if required by the data model. Indices are then created to optimize query access times. End users submit multidimensional analyses to the ROLAP engine, which then dynamically transforms the requests into SQL execution plans. The SQL is submitted to the relational database for processing, the relational query results are cross-tabulated, and a multidimensional result set is returned to the end user. ROLAP is a fully dynamic architecture capable of utilizing pre-calculated results when they are available, or dynamically generating results from atomic information when necessary.

The ROLAP architecture was invented to directly access data from data warehouses, and therefore supports optimization techniques to meet batch window requirements and to provide fast response times. These optimization techniques typically include application-level table partitioning, aggregate inferencing, denormalization support, and multiple fact table joins.

ROLAP is a three-tier, client/server architecture. The database layer utilizes relational databases for data storage, access, and retrieval processes. The application logic layer is the ROLAP engine which executes the multidimensional reports from multiple end users. The ROLAP engine integrates with a variety of presentation layers, through which users perform OLAP analyses.

Framework for Analysis

The objective of this section is to define an analytical framework which can be used to compare the two OLAP architectures. In addition, the key requirements for OLAP are considered and used to define an *OLAP Requirements State-Space* within which to map the capabilities of the two architectures.

As outlined previously, OLAP systems need to (1) support sophisticated analyses, (2) scale to large numbers of dimensions, and (3) support analyses against large atomic data sets. Both ROLAP and MD-OLAP architectures are capable of similar levels of analytical functionality (e.g., multidimensional ratios, comparisons, and ranking). MD-OLAP accomplishes this functionality by primarily accessing stored metrics. ROLAP accomplishes this by using stored metrics if available or by calculating metrics if necessary.

Dimensionality (the number of orthogonal dimensions) and atomicity (amount of atomic data) are the other primary attributes of OLAP applications. The ability of MD-OLAP and ROLAP architectures to handle these two attributes forms the basis of the comparison between the architectures. The two attributes define the OLAP Requirements State-Space, as shown in Figure 7. The MD-OLAP and ROLAP architectures will be mapped onto this state space in the *Comparison of Approaches* section.

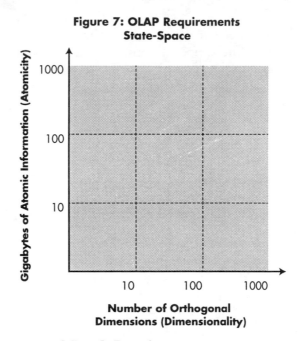

Figure 7: OLAP Requirements State-Space

Query Performance and Batch Requirements

OLAP reports display information at both the base level and at higher consolidated levels. When data needs to be consolidated, OLAP systems can either calculate these values dynamically or retrieve them from a pre-calculated data store. To provide the required performance, OLAP systems typically pre-calculate some (or all) of these values. For example, daily information may be summed during the batch process and the resulting monthly values stored in the database, and retrieved when a month-level report is requested. As is evident, the degree of data compilation is proportional to the batch processing requirements: the more compilation that is required, the larger the batch processing requirements become.

As shown in Figure 8, data passes through a series of steps during the batch process:

- Atomic data is extracted from the transactional systems and stored.

- Atomic data is aggregated.

- Both atomic- and aggregate-level data are indexed for quick retrieval.

Figure 8: Data Compilation Process

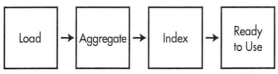

Data passes through a series of processes before it is ready for OLAP analysis.

The series of database designs for OLAP fall on a spectrum, ranging from no compilation (0%) to a fully aggregated and fully indexed data structure (100% compilation). The vast majority of the designs fall in the center of the spectrum. (See sidebar, *Varying Degrees of Compilation*, for further discussion.)

Varying Degrees of Compilation

0% to 15% Compilation

Databases with very little compilation, including transaction-based schemas, fall into this cate-gory. While there are only minimal resource requirements for compila-tion, the resource requirements and response times for run-time queries are high. The basic star schema with one central fact table and lookup tables for each orthogonal dimension is an example of a data model that falls in this compilation range.

15% to 85% Compilation

The goal with sparsely aggregated schemas is to achieve the greatest benefit for the least amount of work. By creating just the aggre-gate tables that people frequently reference, response times are fast on the majority of queries. Additional-ly, indices are placed on those keys which are expected to be referenced frequently. Examples of data models that fall in this category include sparsely aggregated snowflake and star schemas.

85% to 100% Compilation

For those applications with query performance as the primary goal, fully aggregated and fully indexed designs are used. By including every possible aggregate and every possible index, the data model ensures that query response times will always be fast. Of course, these data models require the highest degree of processing requirements for the compilation process. Examples include fully aggregated and fully indexed snowflake schemas, and proprietary structures utilized by multidimensional database servers.

Diminishing Marginal Returns of Data Compilation

As shown in Figures 9 and 10, batch processing requirements increase and query processing requirements decrease with the degree of compilation.

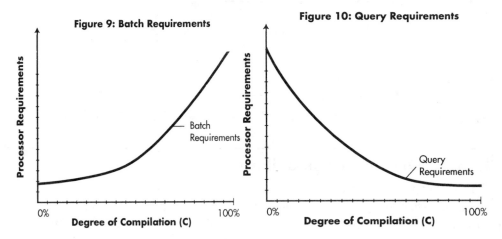

The relationship between the degree of compilation and the resource requirements is nonlinear for batch processing and run-time query execution. There are diminishing marginal returns for each incremental increase in the degree of compilation. Consequently, a small degree of compilation requires the least amount of batch processing and generates the highest degree of performance gains during run time. In our example case, simply calculating a small number of aggregate tables and indexing the most frequently used dimensions (~30% compilation) provided the largest incremental reduction in query response times for end users (~60% shorter). Similarly, the last 5% reduction in response times required the single largest incremental increase in batch resource requirements.

Defining a Systems Analysis Framework

As shown in Figure 11, by combining the *Batch Requirements and Query Requirements* curves, we can derive a *Total Requirements* curve which denotes the combined processing requirements for both run-time and batch operations.

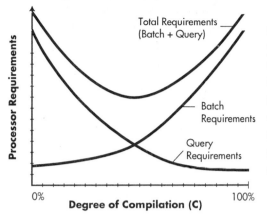

Figure 11: Total Requirements

Processor Requirements (vertical axis)

Total Requirements (Batch + Query)

Batch Requirements

Query Requirements

0%　**Degree of Compilation (C)**　100%

In Figure 12, we add the maximum available level of processing resources of the server, denoted by a horizontal line (Maximum Resources). Of course, an increase or decrease in the power of the server hardware will have the effect of shifting the maximum available processing resources up or down, respectively.

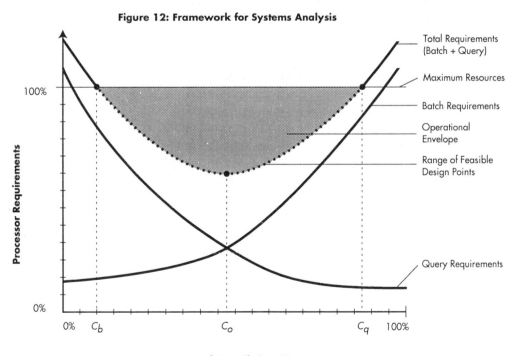

Figure 12: Framework for Systems Analysis

Processor Requirements (vertical axis)

Total Requirements (Batch + Query)

Maximum Resources

Batch Requirements

Operational Envelope

Range of Feasible Design Points

Query Requirements

100%

0%

0%　C_b　C_o　C_q　100%

Degree of Compilation (C)

The Case for Relational OLAP　91

As the range of feasible design points for an OLAP system is constrained by the available processing resources and total processor requirements, it is defined by the *Maximum Resources* curve and the *Total Requirements* curve. The dashed line signifies this range, and is labeled *Range of Feasible Design Points*. From this, we can infer:

- C_b: Compilation point to minimize batch requirements.

- C_q: Compilation point to achieve highest query performance.

- C_o: Optimal point to balance query performance versus batch requirements.

Note: C_b and C_q exist at 100% CPU utilization. C_o provides the largest buffer of computing resources. Other compilation points on the *Range of Feasible Design Points* also provide a buffer of computing resources for fluctuations in system parameters. The buffer area is shaded and is labeled *Operational Envelope*.

What variables affect the design of an OLAP system?

There are five independent variables that have a direct effect on the above curves and design points:

- *Server hardware*: Increasing the processing power will raise the *Maximum Resources* curve enabling greater design flexibility. Decreasing the processing power will have the opposite effect.

- *Query demand*: A more sophisticated or more frequently utilized query profile will raise the *Query Requirements* curve, effectively reducing the *Operational Envelope* and constraining the database design flexibility of the system. A less sophisticated or less active query demand profile will achieve the opposite effect.

- *Number of dimensions*: Increasing the dimensional complexity of the system will raise the *Total Requirements* curve by increasing the batch requirements and query requirements. Decreasing the complexity will have the opposite effect.

- *Atomic data volume*: Increasing the amount of atomic data will increase the processing time required for all operations, and therefore will raise the *Total Requirements* curve and reduce the design flexibility. Decreasing the data volume will have the opposite effect.

- *Data volatility*: If the aggregation rules for atomic data change frequently or users can create their own custom aggregations, the *Batch Requirements* curve will be much steeper. Similarly, a system with low data volatility (stable aggregation structure, no user-defined consolidations) will have a flatter *Batch Requirements* curve. In the high volatility case, the designer will have a smaller *Operational Envelope* than in the low volatility case.

Of these five variables, changes in the volume of atomic data, hardware capabilities, data volatility, and end-user demand all have linear effects on the curves. Dimensionality has an exponential effect on processing requirements as degree of compilation increases. (See Addendum B for a detailed discussion of this relationship.)

The possible profiles for server hardware and end-user query demand are too numerous and distinct to be examined in this paper. In addition, they will have the same effect on both OLAP architectures, and do not provide valuable differentiation points. For this reason, the focus is on how each architecture is equipped to handle data volatility and scale to large numbers of dimensions and large volumes of atomic data.

Comparison of Approaches

Having established a framework for analysis and the state space for comparison, the two architectures can now be evaluated on their ability to meet the OLAP needs of an enterprise.

Degree of Data Compilation

There is a significant difference in the design philosophy of the two OLAP architectures. The ROLAP architecture uses a relational database (RDBMS) for data storage and retrieval, while the MD-OLAP architecture uses a multidimensional database (MDDB). Figure 13 displays a comparison of the two database architectures. RDBMSes support a host of features that enable both quick retrieval of data as well as dynamic compilation of data.

These features include joins, star joins, complex predicates, parallel data queries, etc. ROLAP systems, therefore, tend to be neutral to the degree of data compilation, giving the system designer the ability to decide where to balance query requirements and batch requirements.

**Figure 13: Comparison of Relational
and Multidimensional Databases**

	RDBMS	MDDB
Joins	✓	
Dynamic Consolidation	✓	
Complex Predicates	✓	
Table Scans	✓	
Star Joins	✓	
Data Partitioning	✓	
Parallel Data Querying	✓	
Bitmap Indices	✓	
Hashing	✓	✓
Indexing	✓	✓
Batch Consolidation	✓	✓

In contrast, MDDBs are optimized for data retrieval, hence the heavy focus on hashing and batch consolidations. The philosophy of the MDDB architect is to maximize query performance through greater pre-aggregation of data. While some MD-OLAP tools allow lower data compilation, the underlying database cannot provide acceptable levels of query performance at these compilation levels. Thus, the great majority of MD-OLAP architectures gravitate to data models with high degrees of compilation, typically in the 85% to 100% range.

There is no "silver bullet" approach to data retrieval. Query performance can be improved by increasing the degree of data compilation, which increases batch processing requirements. ROLAP is neutral towards compilation, leaving the decision to the system designer. MD-OLAP is biased towards high degrees of data compilation.

Data Volatility

Volatility describes the degree to which data and data structures change over time. Data with a low level of volatility remains relatively constant. For example, time data typically has a low level of volatility: specific days are always grouped into months, and months are always grouped into years. In contrast, product, employee, and operations data can be highly volatile. Employees change jobs, equipment shifts to perform different functions, and products change categories. It is not uncommon for retailers to intentionally update their item-level groupings on a daily basis in order to increase profitability.

Data volatility adversely affects the batch requirements of the system. Each time atomic data elements change, summarized data that has been precalculated in the batch process needs to be re-calculated. Therefore, volatile data has a greater impact on a highly compiled system, which contains a large quantity of summarized information, than on a system with a low degree of compilation, which calculates summarized values at run time.

Low Volatility

Figure 14 illustrates a system with a low level of volatility. Data elements remain fairly constant, and summarized data does not require frequent recalculation. Given the available *Operational Envelope*, a highly compiled system is advisable and will provide fast response times. Both ROLAP and MD-OLAP are viable options for systems with low data volatility.

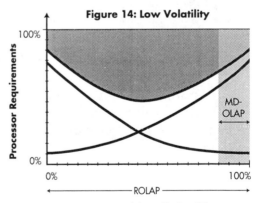

The Case for Relational OLAP 95

High Volatility

Figure 15 illustrates the effects of high volatility on a system. Summarized data must be recalculated frequently; therefore, batch requirements at high degrees of compilation are greatly increased. Full compilation cannot be achieved with a highly volatile system, as all of the system resources are required for recalculating the summarized data. MD-OLAP, which favors high degrees of compilation, is not a viable solution. A ROLAP system, which is neutral to the degree of compilation, is the only choice for a system with high data volatility.

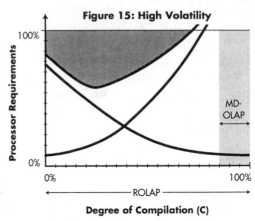

ROLAP systems can be implemented at any degree of compilation and are therefore well suited to handle systems with high data volatility. MD-OLAP requires a high degree of compilation and is not a viable option for systems with volatile data.

Dimensionality: Scaling to Many Dimensions

The following three examples illustrate the effects of increasing the dimensionality of the data model and the ability of ROLAP and MD-OLAP to scale to high levels of dimensionality. Representative examples of systems with the following levels of dimensionality are detailed in Addendum C.

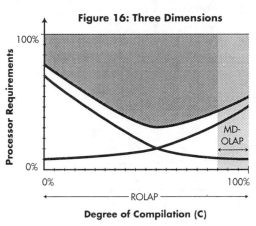

Figure 16: Three Dimensions

Three Dimensions (Figure 16)

With three dimensions in the data model, the batch requirements are relatively low. Total processing requirements are easily met for any design point at any degree of compilation. Given adequate resources, it would be advisable to have a high degree of data compilation to provide fast response times. In this case, either architecture would work for a three-dimensional data model.

Ten Dimensions (Figure 17)

The data model with ten dimensions requires greater processing requirements for the batch processes as degree of compilation increases. Full 100% compilation is no longer attainable. A database design with 85% to 90% compilation is feasible but carries with it the risk that a change in user query demand could "max out" the server. While technically feasible, a MD-OLAP system is not an appropriate choice for this type of data model. A ROLAP system with 50% to 60% compilation would be the appropriate choice.

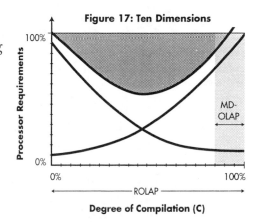

Figure 17: Ten Dimensions

Thirty Dimensions (Figure 18)

The data model with thirty dimensions is well beyond the scope of a MD-OLAP system because the time required to compile the multidimensional database is much greater than the available processor time. The only feasible choice for this data model is a ROLAP system with low compilation.

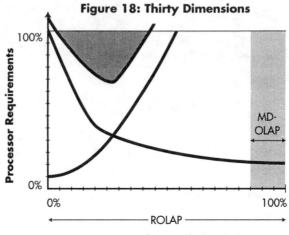

Figure 18: Thirty Dimensions

The ROLAP architecture is better equipped to handle large numbers of dimensions than the MD-OLAP architecture. In addition, by providing a larger operational envelope in all cases, ROLAP is better equipped to deal with fluctuating query-demand profiles.

Atomicity: Scaling to Large Data Volumes

For a given amount of atomic data, the degree of compilation is the main determinant of database size. The more the atomic data is compiled into higher aggregation levels, the larger the size of the database becomes. In Addendum B, we can see that the expansion factors for fully compiled data models are nontrivial. For example, the expansion factor for a fully compiled, five-dimensional model is 32. Thus, a database with 300 megabytes of atomic information would result in a database of 9.6 gigabytes, and a database with 20 gigabytes of atomic information would result in a database of 640 gigabytes. A highly compiled data model becomes unfeasible as the amount of atomic data increases (this phenomenon is only compounded when the system becomes dimensionally more complex). Given MD-OLAP's bias towards highly compiled data models, it eliminates itself from consideration when large volumes (10+ gigabytes) of atomic data are involved.

ROLAP's neutrality towards data compilation allows system designers to implement sparsely aggregated database designs. The expansion factors are much smaller for lower degrees of compilation, and even large amounts of atomic data can be accessed within user-acceptable time frames.

Expansion in a Multidimensional Database

In one benchmark published by a multidimensional database vendor, an eight-dimensional data model with a 57-megabyte sample of real-world input information expanded to 43 gigabytes in the final multidimensional database. While 57 megabytes is a useful test sample, a larger volume of input information fully illustrates the limitations of the multidimensional approach. Imagine the database size with 5 gigabytes of input data.

The ROLAP architecture is better equipped to handle large data volumes than the MD-OLAP architecture. By not requiring fully compiled data models and by utilizing aggregate inferencing, parallel processing, and partitioning technologies, ROLAP systems can scale to large volumes of atomic data.

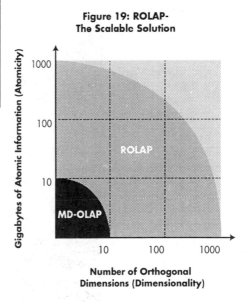

Figure 19: ROLAP-The Scalable Solution

ROLAP is the Scaleable Architecture

As shown in Figure 19, when both architectures are mapped to the OLAP Requirements State-Space, it becomes very clear that ROLAP is capable of scaling far beyond the limits of MD-OLAP in terms of large numbers of dimensions and large volumes of data.

Do organizations need the power of ROLAP?

Scaling to large volumes of data is critical to supporting the majority of OLAP and decision support applications. Merchant retail systems on average have 100+ gigabyte volumes of input data, well beyond the compiled limits of a multidimensional database. Banking applications typically have smaller volumes of data but extremely high dimensionality, including hundreds of characteristics by which the data needs to be analyzed and aggregated. ROLAP scales to meet this need, while MD-OLAP is limited to 5-10 dimensions. The large volumes of data and the high dimensionality of certain market segmentation applications even stress the current limits of ROLAP, and are multiple orders of magnitude beyond the limits of multidimensional databases. Figure 20 maps forty business applications to the *OLAP Requirements State-Space*.

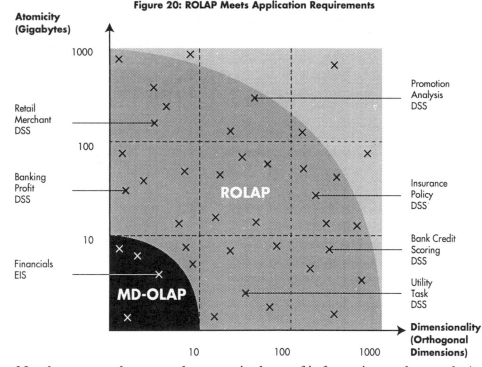

Figure 20: ROLAP Meets Application Requirements

Nearly everyone has more than ten gigabytes of information and more than ten dimensions. ROLAP is the only architecture capable of meeting these application requirements.

Conclusion

To meet business requirements, OLAP systems need to (1) support sophisticated analyses, (2) scale to large numbers of dimensions, and (3) support analyses against large atomic data sets. ROLAP systems and MD-OLAP systems are both capable of providing analytically sophisticated reports and analysis functionality. It is the latter two requirements that fundamentally differentiate the two OLAP architectures.

All OLAP systems must make a trade-off between the degree of batch compilation and run-time query performance. To be effective, the MD-OLAP architecture requires a high degree of compilation, while the ROLAP architecture allows systems with any degree of compilation. This difference severely limits the ability of MD-OLAP to scale to highly volatile systems, highly dimensional data models, or large volumes of data.

For small data volumes with similar degrees of compilation, ROLAP provides generally comparable performance to that of MD-OLAP systems. For large data volumes, the batch requirements of MD-OLAP preclude it from being a viable solution. ROLAP is suitable for large data volumes and typically supports data retrieval optimization strategies. ROLAP systems are aligned with the industry-standard relational database technology, while MD-OLAP relies on a proprietary multidimensional database technology.

ROLAP is a flexible, general architecture that scales to meet a wide variety of DSS and OLAP needs. MD-OLAP is a particular solution that is suitable for departmental systems with small data volumes and limited dimensionality.

Notes

Chapter 5, Addendum A

Dispelling OLAP Myths

—MicroStrategy, Inc.

Myth: *Data has to be stored multidimensionally to be viewed multidimensionally.*

Relational OLAP allows the multidimensional analysis of information stored in a relational database.

Fact: *Data can be viewed multidimensionally even when stored in a relational format.*

Myth: *ROLAP has slower performance than MD-OLAP.*

A fully aggregated and fully indexed relational database provides equivalent performance to that of any multidimensional database. ROLAP allows system implementors to make the design trade-offs between end-user query performance, database compilation time, database size, and database maintainability. In contrast, the MD-OLAP architecture always forces developers to maximize end-user query speed at the expense of the other parameters. Thus, when the data model is fully compiled, ROLAP performance matches MD-OLAP systems on small data sets. Due to MD-OLAP's inability to scale above small data volumes, ROLAP will always outperform a MD-OLAP system on large data sets.

Fact: *ROLAP matches MD-OLAP performance for small data sets. MD-OLAP cannot access large data sets.*

Myth: *ROLAP systems require developers and end users to write SQL.*

ROLAP systems utilize a query generation engine that dynamically translates end-user multidimensional analysis requests into performance-optimized SQL execution plans. The sophisticated multidimensional reports found in many OLAP applications certainly translate into complex SQL execution plans; however, the end users are completely removed from the SQL writing process and never see the SQL that is submitted to the relational database. Any decision support application that does not automatically generate SQL based on multidimensional analysis requests is an ad hoc data viewer and not a ROLAP system.

Fact: *All the SQL in ROLAP architectures is generated dynamically and transparently.*

Myth: *SQL is not capable of the sophisticated analytical functionality necessary for OLAP.*

While the more complex calculations are not possible using a single SQL statement, the ROLAP engine generates SQL execution plans with multiple SQL statements. A multi-pass query can very easily generate the full range of calculations necessary for business analysis. Figure i compares the analytical sophistication of ROLAP and MD-OLAP systems.

**Figure i: ROLAP Provides
Superior Analytical Capabilities**

	ROLAP	MD-OLAP
Calculated Metrics	✓	✓
Simple Ratios and Ranks	✓	✓
Period Comparisons	✓	✓
Basket Analysis	✓	
Filtered Comparisons	✓	
Ad Hoc Segmentation	✓	
Financial Consolidations	✓	✓
Beginning/Ending Stock	✓	✓
Variance Analysis	✓	✓
Forecasting	✓	✓

Fact: *Theoretically and practically, ROLAP systems are more capable than MD-OLAP of generating all the metrics needed for business analysis.*

Myth: *ROLAP requires large amounts of data to be moved over the network.*

ROLAP calculations are always performed using SQL on the relational database and never require or utilize additional programs on separate platforms to perform these calculations. In general, the most powerful hardware in the ROLAP system is the platform for the relational database. Performing calculations through SQL on the relational database provides two advantages: (1) the powerful server hardware performs calculations in the shortest amount of time and (2) network traffic is minimized because only result sets, not unprocessed data, are transferred to client machines.

Fact: ROLAP does all of the processing on the RDBMS; only result sets are transferred across the network.

Myth: *ROLAP provides limited application functionality.*

A comprehensive set of analysis capabilities is available with ROLAP systems for stream-of-consciousness navigation and workflow automation. Relational OLAP provides the complete range of drill-down, drill-up, and data pivoting capabilities. The more advanced systems provide intelligent agents, which enable the automation of recurring groups of reports and the ability to scan the data warehouse for exceptions by using alerts.

The relational architecture and data access using SQL provide some analytical advantages over the multidimensional database technology. ROLAP enables the use of advanced filtering objects, which are difficult or impossible to utilize with a multidimensional database. Using set math, end users can easily define and embed any set of limiting criteria. Data surfing is a capability unique to ROLAP that enables true stream-of-consciousness navigation, by allowing end users to progressively define and refine their analyses using filtering objects.

Fact: The ROLAP architecture is functionally richer than MD-OLAP.

Myth: *MD-OLAP can scale to large numbers of dimensions.*

As illustrated in the *Comparison of Approaches* section of this chapter, MD-OLAP is severely limited in the number of dimensions it can support. Because multidimensional databases are biased towards full compilation for all dimen-sions, the calculation and storage requirements increase at an exponential rate with the number of dimensions. Consequently, multidimensional databases are limited to a very small levels of dimensionality.

Fact: MD-OLAP is only viable for simple dimensional models.

Myth: *Multidimensional databases are a proven technology.*

The multidimensional database technology has demonstrated none of the success found with relational databases. Relational databases have had proven success with terabytes of atomic data. Multidimensional databases rarely implement systems that scale above five gigabytes of atomic information. Worldwide, there are over 100,000 certified professionals who are capable of supporting relational databases. In contrast, there is no standard for multidimensional databases. Developers proficient in one vendor's system will have great difficulty transferring their knowledge to a different vendor's system.

**Figure ii: Relational Databases-
The Strategic Choice**

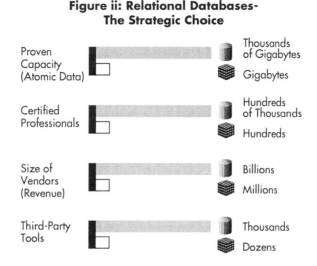

Relational databases have demonstrated industry success well beyond the limits of multidimensional databases. Relational databases are the strategic choice for OLAP.

The relational database industry has grown past $10 billion in 1995. The multidimensional database industry is orders of magnitude below this level. This dichotomy provides ROLAP systems with a distinct advantage over MD-OLAP. Aligning with the relational database technology has the added benefit of aligning with thousands of vendors who are producing tools that work with relational databases.

Fact: ROLAP is the proven technology for OLAP.

Myth: ROLAP systems require specialized database schemas.

ROLAP systems are highly flexible and support database schemas ranging from transaction-based systems to fully compiled schemas. Examples of schemas supported by ROLAP include star schemas, snowflake schemas, denormalized and normalized fact tables, sparse and full aggregations, table partitions, redundant data compression, and multiple fact tables.

Fact: ROLAP supports a wide range of database schemas.

Myth: OLAP allows unlimited slicing and dicing.

Multidimensional databases store information in subsegments often called data-cubes or multi-cubes. MD-OLAP typically provides advanced functionality for slicing and dicing information within a specific data-cube. However, slicing and dicing information stored in multiple data-cubes requires an entirely new data-cube to be calculated in a time-consuming and resource-intensive process. This problem cannot occur in a ROLAP system because the information is in a single data store.

Fact: ROLAP allows unlimited slicing and dicing of the data in the warehouse. MD-OLAP faces many technical obstacles before it can enable the same.

Myth: End users don't need access to atomic-level information.

Summarized, high-level data frequently provides a good starting point for decision support analyses, enabling users to identify areas of the business that require attention. However, it is the atomic-level information that allows decision makers to implement actionable solutions. For example, a high-level retail report might identify below plan sales in the Central Region. Then, an atomic-level report is able to pinpoint the cause of the problem to a specific set of goods with low inventory levels in four stores.

Fact: Atomic-level information is essential for making actionable decisions.

Myth: SQL Drill-through provides all the functionality in ROLAP.

SQL Drill-through is the "patch" offered by MD-OLAP vendors to battle the criticisms leveled against the architecture. Generally, either the end users or system developers need to write the SQL required to access specific sections of the relational database. If an end user asks a question about an area for which a preprogrammed SQL query has not been written, then no data can be returned. SQL Drill-through does not provide advanced OLAP metrics against atomic-level data, because the atomic-level data is not physically stored in the multidimensional database (which provides the application logic for multidimensional viewing).

A few MD-OLAP vendors have begun developing rudimentary query engines; however, none of them support table inferencing, many-to-many relations, compound keys, denormalization, split facts, sparse aggregations, physical partitions, set theory, dynamic consolidation, exception scanning, and row math directly against very large data warehouses.

Fact: *SQL Drill-through is an ineffective substitute for true ROLAP.*

Myth: *MD-OLAP can handle many-to-many relationships.*

Many-to-many relationships are hierarchies in which parents have multiple children, and children have multiple parents. For example, many items may be sold in green, and any individual item might come in green as well as blue, orange, red, or brown. Frequently, transaction systems contain many-to-many relationships that are then passed on to the OLAP/DSS application. Multidimensional databases follow a distinct hierarchy structure that uses one-to-one or one-to-many relationships; they are not designed to handle many-to-many relationships.

Fact: *MD-OLAP cannot handle many-to-many relationships.*

Myth: *A published API makes MD-OLAP as open as relational technologies.*

The degree to which an architecture is open is a function of the number of companies, developers, and products that support it in the marketplace. An investment in relational database technology is an investment that is supported by thousands of companies and hundreds of thousands of developers worldwide. ROLAP vendors conform to ANSI-standard SQL for access to relational databases. Multidimensional databases currently follow no standard and are proprietary systems, with a database-specific set of controls. Beyond the original manufacturers, few, if any, companies support the proprietary set of protocols unique to each multidimensional database. A standard API for MD-OLAP might help to increase the level of openness; however, there is a long way to go before MD-OLAP is as open as the corresponding relational technologies.

Fact: *MD-OLAP is a proprietary technology.*

Notes

Chapter 5, Addendum B

The Exponential Effect of Dimensionality on Database Size and Compilation Requirements

—MicroStrategy, Inc.

This addendum presents a qualitative analysis that illustrates the exponential effect of dimensionality on database size and compilation requirements.

Data Expansion in a N-Dimensional Array

As a basic example consider the two-dimensional array in Figure iii. Each dimension contains five base elements and one calculated total element. In the two-dimensional array, the total number of base elements is 25 (5 items x 5 stores = 25), and the total number of calculated elements is 11 (5 item totals + 5 store totals + 1 grand total = 11).

For one dimension, the expansion factor is 1.2 (6 elements / 5 elements). When the model is expanded to two dimensions, the expansion factor increases to 1.44 (36 elements / 25 elements). This relationship can be expressed as follows for a single dimension, a:

Total number of elements = $K_a C_a$, where

K = number of base elements

C = expansion coefficient

In Figure iii, K_a= 5 elements and C_a = 1.2. The total number of elements in a single dimension is then 5 x 1.2 = 6.

For two dimensions, a and b, where

$K_a = K_b = 5$, and

$C_a = C_b = 1.2$

Total number of elements

$= (K_a C_a)(K_b C_b)$

$= (K_a K_b)(C_a C_b)$

$= (5 \times 5)(1.2 \times 1.2)$

$= (25)(1.44)$

$= 36$

Here, we see that the expansion factor for the two-dimensional model is 1.44. If a third dimension, c, were added to the model, the total number of elements would be expressed as:

Total number of elements

$= (K_a K_b K_c)(C_a C_b C_c)$

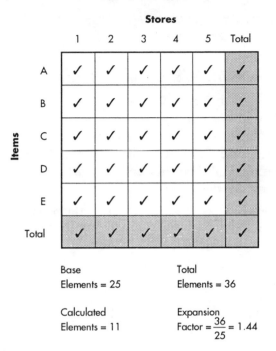

Figure iii: Sample Two-Dimensional Model

Stores

	1	2	3	4	5	Total
A	✓	✓	✓	✓	✓	✓
B	✓	✓	✓	✓	✓	✓
C	✓	✓	✓	✓	✓	✓
D	✓	✓	✓	✓	✓	✓
E	✓	✓	✓	✓	✓	✓
Total	✓	✓	✓	✓	✓	✓

(left axis label: **Items**)

Base Elements = 25   Total Elements = 36

Calculated Elements = 11   Expansion Factor $= \dfrac{36}{25} = 1.44$

Making the assumption that all of the dimensions in the model are identical, the expression can be re-written as:

Total number of elements = $K^n C^n$

K^n describes the quantity of base data, and C^n is the factor that describes the overall increase in the size of the database, due to aggregation. Using the above expression with four dimensions, the overall size of the database would increase by a factor of $C^4 = 1.2^4 = 2.07$.

Total number of elements

$$= 5^4 \times 1.2^4$$

$$= 625 \times 2.07$$

$$= 1296 \text{ elements}$$

The important point to notice about this relationship is that the expansion factor increases exponentially with the number of dimensions. The expansion coefficient, C, is a function of the number of aggregation levels and the degree of consolidation within a dimension.

Increased Expansion With Sparse Data Sets

So far, this analysis has assumed a completely dense set of base data (i.e., each item was sold in every store on every day). While the expansion effects are most easily understood on a dense data set, this is not typical of real-world data. In fact, base data sets are generally highly sparse. In the context of the above example, only a small number of items would actually be sold in a given store on a given day.

Sparse data sets have a much greater degree of expansion than dense data sets. This effect is illustrated in Figure iv. If just one item is sold in a store, then a total for that store needs to be calculated. One base element has expanded into two elements: the original base element and one calculated element. Similarly, if an item is sold in one store, then a total needs to be calculated for that item's sales. Because just one base element is required to create an aggregate element, aggregate entries in a data set are typically very dense.

In Figure iv, just 6 elements of base data translate into a total of 17 elements in

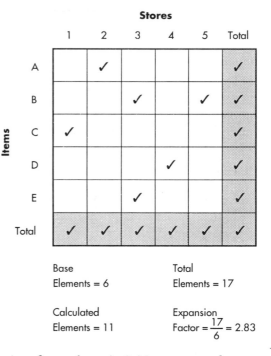

Figure iv: Sparse Two-Dimensional Model

Base Elements = 6

Calculated Elements = 11

Total Elements = 17

Expansion Factor $= \dfrac{17}{6} = 2.83$

the calculated data set. The expansion factor here is 2.83, a tremendous increase from the 1.44 factor in the model with dense base data.

Due to the fact that aggregate levels are typically dense, sparsity serves to amplify the overall increase in the size of the data set and therefore the expansion coefficient, C. This relationship can be expressed as follows:

Total number of elements = KC^n, where

K = the quantity of base data

C = the expansion coefficient

n = the number of dimensions

Typically, values for C range from 1.5 to 3.0 depending on the sparsity of the base data set and the number of levels and degree of compression in the aggregate entries.

Conclusion

Figure v illustrates this effect for an expansion coefficient of 2.0. For small numbers of dimensions, the degree of expansion is relatively low. However, as the number of dimensions increases, the exponential effect on data set size becomes increasingly significant.

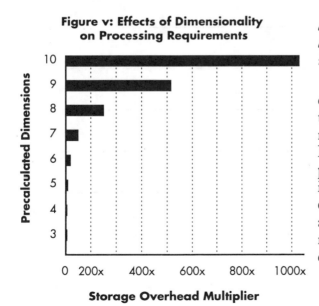

Figure v: Effects of Dimensionality on Processing Requirements

Precalculated Dimensions

Storage Overhead Multiplier

As the number of dimensional increases, the database expansion factor increases exponentially.

The resulting size of the data set translates to far more than additional disk and memory requirements. Processing requirements are proportional to the increase in the size of the data set, as each calculated data value is an additional calculation that must be performed by the database.

Notes

Chapter 5, Addendum C

Examples of OLAP Systems with Different Numbers of Dimensions

—MicroStrategy, Inc.

Sample of 3 Dimensional Hierarchies for Manufacturing
- Manufacturing Year–Quarter–Week
- Region–Distributor–Retailer
- Full System–Components–Parts

Sample of 10 Dimensional Hierarchies for Retail
- Division–Department–Class–Item
- Region–Market–Store
- Year–Quarter–Month–Date
- State–City–Zip Code–Customer
- Color–Item
- Promotion Period–Date
- Store Type–Store
- Gender–Customer
- Size–Item
- Demography–Customer

Sample of 30 Dimensional Hierarchies for Insurance
- Customer–Policy
- Company–Policy
- Financial Coverage–Coverage–Coverage
  Multiplier–Policy Detail
- Risk Type–Policy
- Rate Method–Policy
- Coverage Status–Policy
- Financial Responsibility–Policy
- Contract Type–Policy
- Policy Expiration Date–Policy

- Rate Set–Policy
- Financial Location–Policy Base Location–Policy
- Assigned Risk Plan–Vehicle Policy
- Facility Code–Vehicle Policy
- Policy Effective Period–Vehicle Policy
- Policy Type–Vehicle Policy
- Town Code–Vehicle Policy
- Assigned Risk Surcharge–Vehicle Policy
- Amount of Insurance–Property Policy
- Property Country–Property City–
  Property Zip Code–Property Policy
- Earthquake Zone–Property Policy
- Fire Protection Code–Property Policy
- Construction Type Rate–Property Policy
- Seasonal Rate–Property Policy
- Security Device Discount–Property Policy
- New Home Discount Percent–Property Policy
- Distance to Fire Department–Property Policy
- Distance to Fire Hydrant–Property Policy
- Number of Families in Residence–Property Policy
- Number of Units per Building–Property Policy
- Number of Units between Fire Walls–Property Policy

Note: These examples do not specify a generic industry model. A retail or a manufacturing system could easily have 20 or 30 dimensions. Similarly, a basic insurance system might have just a few dimensions.

Further Reading

Data Warehouse Query Tools: Evolving to Relational OLAP
Aberdeen Group Research Note
Volume 8/Number 8, July 7, 1995

Major Changes Ahead for OLAP: Buyers Beware
Gartner Group Research Note
November 9, 1994, SPA-OLAP-1331

Data, Data Everywhere
Information Week
Neil Raden
October 30, 1995, p. 60

True Relational OLAP: The Future of Decision Support
Database Journal
Michael J. Saylor, Manish G. Acharya, and
Robert G. Trenkamp
November/December 1995, p. 38

Polishing Sales with OLAP
Open Computing
Larry Stevens
December 1995, p. 71

Chapter 6

Specialized Requirements for Relational Data Warehouse Servers

—Red Brick Systems

Introduction

Businesses in virtually every industry are deploying data warehouse systems. Data warehouses bring together large volumes of quantitative business information obtained from transaction processing and legacy operational systems. The information is cleaned and transformed so that it is complete and reliable, and is collected and retained over time so that changes and trends can be identified.

In many data warehouse applications, the information is made directly available to managers and business analysts through client/server networks and powerful query and analysis tools. In other applications, data warehouses work together with operational applications in a "closed loop" system performing information-driven functions such as intelligent inventory reordering.

The data warehouse was originally envisioned as a single enterprise-scale "data tank" containing "everything about everything." More commonly today, data warehouses are subject-oriented and designed and built to address specific business needs. Enterprises typically deploy multiple data warehouses with different data, different summary levels, and different user communities.

A production data warehouse system consists of many components including client analysis and reporting tools, legacy and transaction data extraction subsystems and metadata management tools. However, the most important single component of a data warehouse system is the Relational Database Management System (RDBMS) server used to store vast quantities of information and to quickly and reliably answer a wide range of business questions.

Just as on-line transaction processing (OLTP) environments demand specialized technologies to satisfy application demands, data warehouse environments require equally specialized technologies. OLTP systems demand ever-increasing performance, where the state-of-the-art is now well beyond 1000 transactions per second. Data warehouse environments require a similar focus on performance, but the performance demands are quite different. A single query on a large database can require thousands or millions of times more work (and different work at that) than a typical OLTP transaction. Moreover, data warehouse systems are required to support tens to hundreds of concurrent query operations of this intensity.

In addition to needing high performance, OLTP systems require specialized functionality to address the transaction workload such as triggers, transaction monitors and rollback logging. Similarly specialized functionality is required for data warehouse systems.

This white paper looks beyond the obvious requirements for any modern database system such as open client/server access, ANSI standard

SQL, and multiprocessor support. It examines requirements in ten areas in which the data warehouse RDBMS server must provide specialized performance and functionality.

LOAD PERFORMANCE

LOAD PROCESSING

DATA QUALITY MANAGEMENT

QUERY PERFORMANCE

TERABYTE SCALABILITY

MASS USER SCALABILITY

NETWORKED DATA WAREHOUSE

WAREHOUSE ADMINISTRATION

INTEGRATED DIMENSIONAL ANALYSIS

ADVANCED QUERY FUNCTIONALITY

Warehouse Server Requirements

1. Load Performance

Data warehouse updates are frequently very large— tens of gigabytes (GBs) and hundreds of millions of rows— and usually must be accomplished within narrow batch windows. For example, point-of-sale detail records are often captured daily and must be loaded and prepared for use in the space of a few overnight hours. New applications and added levels of detail increase the size and frequency of updates, but do not add more hours to the day in which to accomplish them.

As a result, extremely fast update performance is critical to data warehouse success and growth. The "loader" subsystem of the RDBMS must be able to perform complete data loading and preparation including format conversion, integrity enforcement and indexing, and it must accomplish all of these steps at rates measured in hundreds of millions of rows and gigabytes per hour. To minimize elapsed time and fit short batch windows, the RDBMS loader must effectively utilize all system resources including being able to harness and apply the entire processing power of a large parallel processor system.

In the event of a failure, recovery and restart processes must be equally fast. Recovery and restart must be accomplished within minutes so that the full update can complete within a narrow batch window.

2. Load Processing

Virtually all of the data stored in a data warehouse originates in external systems. Examples include retail point-of-sale data collected from store systems, telephone call detail records from switching centers, purchased data such as government census records and corporate transaction data from inventory, manufacturing, financial and other systems. Getting this data into the data warehouse and fully preparing it for use is the key update in a data warehouse system.

In most data warehouses, updates work with batches of data, and occur on a periodic, scheduled basis such as daily or weekly. Batches can be very large— up to ten gigabytes and beyond— and can contain tens or hundreds of millions of new or updated records.

Many steps are required to transform raw external source data into information ready for end-user access and business decision making:

- The data must be read directly from a variety of feeds including disk files, network feeds, mainframe channel connections and magnetic tapes;
- The data must be converted to the database internal format from a variety of external representations including fixed and variable length records, character and binary formats, IBM EBCDIC data, packed decimal, zoned decimal, etc.;
- The data must be filtered to reject invalid data values, duplicate keys or otherwise erroneous records;
- Records must be reorganized from external flat-file representations to match the relational schema of the data warehouse;
- Records must be checked against the existing database to ensure table-level and global consistency and to maintain complete referential integrity;

- Records must be written to physical storage observing configuration requirements for data segmentation, physical device placement, inter-disk balancing, etc.;
- Records must be fully and richly indexed; and,
- System metadata must be updated.

A data warehouse update is not complete until all of these steps have been accomplished successfully. This requires a loading and data preparation tool which conducts all of these activities as a unified process and which provides the necessary administrative controls and recovery facilities.

As with OLTP transactions, data warehouse updates require methods for recovery and restart in the event of an error or a system failure. Traditional OLTP recovery approaches fail to meet this requirement because they depend on transaction logs and rollback mechanisms which are unable to accommodate the record counts and data volumes involved in typical data warehouse updates. Specialized recovery and restart techniques are required in the database to support data warehouse updates.

3. Data Quality Management

The insights gained from a data warehouse can only be as good as the quality of the information stored in the warehouse, yet source data feeds are often "dirty" and unpredictable. The data warehouse server must provide mechanisms to clean and filter input data, and must provide mechanisms to continuously guarantee overall data quality.

In the context of data warehouse applications, local consistency requires that each individual data item be valid and meaningful, and global consistency requires that various data items across the warehouse be self-consistent. For example, it would be a local consistency error if "Saskatchewan" were to appear in a table containing names of U.S. states, or if a negative value were to appear in a table tracking current inventory. It might be a global consistency error if sales data from western region stores were missing for the July 25 period from the point-of-sale transaction detail table. The database server must enforce local consistency and detect discrepancies from overall global consistency.

Data warehouse schemas almost always contain multiple tables which reference each other and which are brought together and matched using SQL join operations to answer queries. For example, a column containing a customer ID number in a transaction detail table might reference a matching customer ID number column in a customer information table. Accurate query results depend on all inter-table references being valid at all times, a property called *referential integrity*. The database server must enforce referential integrity at all times and must not allow dirty data or incorrect updates to breach total referential integrity. Referential integrity must be checked and enforced during load updates, SQL DELETE operations and any other operation which changes data in the warehouse.

4. Query Performance

Data warehouse applications range from highly-interactive *ad hoc* analysis systems to complex information-driven operational systems supporting such business-critical activities as inventory management and pricing.

Truly effective interactive query applications require near real-time performance. End-user analysts need to be able to fluidly ask questions, get answers and ask follow-up questions at a pace matching their own thought processes. They need to be able to pursue different lines of inquiry, to look at information from different perspectives and to drill up and down through different levels of detail. In this environment, query response times measured in minutes or hours are unacceptable. Analysts' thought processes are interrupted, and the costs of creative exploration of the information resource are too great to be practical. Interactive query applications require response times measured in seconds, independent of the level of detail and the size of the database, and this performance level must be maintained in multi-user environments.

At the other end of the response time spectrum are extremely complex operational queries driven off millions or even billions of rows of detail data. These query intensive applications often form a "closed loop" with operational business systems and can initiate a series of business activities without end-user intervention. For example, a "closed loop" application might perform intelligent inventory replenishment based on past sales data, or select target customer pools based on market-basket or purchase history data. Extremely fast query performance is required even to begin to make this class of sophisticated applications practical. It is impossible to perform daily inventory reordering based on a query that runs for three days. For this category of applications, even the largest queries on the largest databases must complete within a few minutes to a few hours.

These application performance requirements translate directly onto the data warehouse server. The data warehouse RDBMS must include query performance optimizations analogous to those that have yielded OLTP performance of thousands of transactions per second. In the warehouse environment, performance optimizations must comprehensively address the computationally-intensive aspects of query processing such as joins, sorting and grouping.

5. Terabyte Scalability

Although most data warehouses today range from a few gigabytes up to several hundred gigabytes, data warehouse sizes are growing rapidly and many users foresee the near-term need for data warehouses in excess of one terabyte. This astonishing growth is driven by the increased storage of detailed transaction-level data (e.g., point-of-sale, credit charge, call detail record, etc.), storage of data for longer periods of time (e.g., five-year history), and cross-functional integration of data (e.g., incorporation of sales, shipment, inventory, and financial data in the same data warehouse).

Not only are data warehouses large in aggregate, but some individual tables are huge. The data warehouse RDBMS must routinely support detail data tables containing one to two billion records or more.

Large-scale data warehouses impose many specialized requirements on a relational database system.

- At the most basic level, the RDBMS must not have any architectural limits near the application's size requirements. The server must be able to address and manage many terabytes of physical storage, and must be able to successfully process tables with many billions of rows. All database operations— joins, aggregations, sorts, indexing, etc.— must be fully supported on tables of this size.

- Database administrator (DBA) activities which are routine on a five GB database quickly become prohibitive on a terabyte-scale database. A simple database reorganization which would require 45 minutes on a five GB database requires almost a week to complete on a terabyte database! Clearly, the large-scale data warehouse database must take a different approach to storage management and administration:

   a. First, the database must eliminate entirely the need for all but a few storage management activities. It is not adequate to try to accelerate a one-week data reorganization so that it completes in four days; the database must never require a data reorganization at all.

   b. For those DBA activities which remain, the database must support modular and parallel management. Modular management means it must be possible to perform DBA activities such as unload, backup, and restore against just a part of a table at a time while maintaining global consistency. Parallel management means it must be possible to apply the same management operation to different parts of the database at the same time on a multiprocessor system.

- With today's hardware technology, a terabyte database requires 500 to 1,000 or more physical disk drives, plus up to 100 or more disk controllers and associated hardware. Even with excellent hardware reliability, hardware failures are inevitable. The database must support continued availability in the face of a point failure; it must be possible for users to continue to access unaffected parts of the database, and even continue to access a single table, while the affected part is repaired and recovered.

- A very large warehouse database requires a fundamentally different approach to managing recovery from failure. Traditional OLTP systems create large journal or log files containing images of changed data. These logs are carefully managed, and in the event of a failure are used to restore the database to its prior state. This technique works well when the database is small and transactions change only a few records at a time. However, in the data warehouse, updates can be extremely large. A single load process might place hundreds of millions of new records into the database, occupying several gigabytes or more. A single UPDATE might affect hundreds of millions of rows, and an ALTER TABLE ADD COLUMN statement might update every row in a two-billion row table.

- Clearly it is impractical to create a transaction log for a single update affecting millions or billions of rows. Large-scale data warehouses require a fundamentally different mechanism for recovery: one that does not depend on preserving a copy of every changed row. Instead, data warehouse RDBMS products must provide for checkpointing and rapid restart of interrupted operations so they may be cleanly and quickly resumed and completed.

- Although it is valuable, older data typically is accessed less frequently than the most current data. It is often desirable to move older historical data to less expensive storage media. To deliver cost-effective storage, data warehouse servers must support on-line mass storage devices such as optical disk, as well as Hierarchical Storage Management (HSM) environments using "juke boxes" and other robotic storage systems. The database server must catalog and track data on off-line devices, and it must provide automated mechanisms for migrating older data to lower-cost optical and other HSM devices. The server must allow users transparent access to HSM data by automatically staging and bringing on-line the required data as it is referenced through SQL queries.

- As data warehouses grow, the amount of data required by individual queries does not necessarily grow. It is critical that query performance not be penalized just because of growth in individual tables, in the number of users, or in the database as a whole. The requirement for data warehousing is that query performance be dependent on the complexity of the query, not the size of the database. For example, a query which selects information about product sales in the current month should be completely unaffected by the total number of months of data stored in the warehouse. On the other hand, a query which totals every record in a table would be affected by growing data volumes.

6. Mass User Scalability

Data warehouses and decision support systems are no longer specialized technologies needed by only a few key managers and analysts within an enterprise. Major trends driving the requirement for mass user scalability include:

- Multi-level management hierarchies yielding to flatter organizations;
- Cross-functional organizations requiring access to common data; and,
- Intercompany relationships becoming co-dependent on shared data.

The bottom line is more individuals at more levels in more job functions across more organizations require access to data within a warehouse server. With decision making authority spread out among so many disparate user communities, fact-based decision making becomes imperative.

The need for mass user access to factual business information means that the data warehouse RDBMS server needs to support hundreds and even thousands of concurrent users while maintaining acceptable query performance. This requires that the server:

- Support effective caching and sharing of data to minimize I/O bottlenecks;
- Efficiently task switch among hundreds of currently running queries; and,
- Fully exploit multiple processors and large memories to scale with demand.

With hundreds or thousands of authorized users, it becomes impractical for the DBA to administer each user account on an individual basis. The server must provide for flexibility in administering data access privileges, end-user security controls, performance priorities, etc. to be applied equivalently to individuals or groups of users.

7. Networked Data Warehouse

Data warehouses rarely exist in isolation. Increasingly, multiple data warehouse systems cooperate in a larger network of data warehouses. A large enterprise may have many subject-area warehouses as well as warehouses in different divisions and geographic locations. Warehouses may participate in a hierarchy in which detailed information from several subject-area data warehouses is summarized and consolidated in a corporate data warehouse.

Advanced applications extend warehouse networks across enterprise boundaries. For example, retailers wish to share sales data with suppliers in an integrated warehouse network. Similarly, vendors wish to share information with customers, such as a telecommunications company sharing call detail information with key large-volume customers.

Implementation and management of networks of data warehouses impose new requirements on the warehouse RDBMS. The server must come integrated with tools which coordinate movement of information between warehouses. Just as updates in the warehouse usually involve large periodic batches, the unit of exchange between network warehouses is also usually a batch. This requires tools which define, extract, move and update batches of information as self-consistent units, rather than the "trickle" update provided by OLTP-oriented replication services.

In the network warehouse world, users must be able to look at and work with multiple warehouses from a single client workstation, requiring location transparency across the network. Similarly, warehouse managers must be able to manage and administer a network of warehouses from a single physical location.

8. *Warehouse Administration*

Beyond the rich set of administrative capabilities required of any large-scale relational database management system, data warehouse servers require additional management and administration tools to address specialized needs.

Significant value in a data warehouse comes from the maintenance of consistent historical data. Historical data enables trend analysis and gives users the ability to identify and explore changes in the business over time. Frequently, data warehouses use a time-cyclic structure in which the oldest data is removed from the warehouse as the newest group of data is added.

For example, a retailer may use a 65-week rolling design for a fact table containing point-of-sale information in which the oldest week's worth of data is removed as the current week's sales information is added. To support time-cyclic operations, administration features of the RDBMS must allow time-groupings of data to be named, managed and stored together.

The server must allow time groups to be added to the data warehouse, moved around and removed from the data warehouse using simple specialized operations and without requiring data defragmentation or reorganization.

Individual data warehouse query operations can consume significant system resources, including memory, processor and disk I/O. Query frequency, timing and complexity are generally under the control of end users in a client/server environment. The warehouse administrator needs tools to manage the impact of intensive, concurrent query processing.

In particular, the data warehouse RDBMS must provide controls for implementing resource limits to warn users or terminate queries which consume excessive resources. The system must implement charge-back accounting to allocate query costs back to data warehouse users, and query prioritization to meet the needs of different user classes and activities. Also, the system must provide for workload tracking and tuning mechanisms to enable the DBA to analyze which queries are consuming the most system resources, so that schemas, access paths and disk layouts may be optimized to deliver maximum performance and throughput.

9. Integrated Dimensional Analysis

Most data warehouse applications present the user with a "dimensional" view of the data in which quantitative or other factual information is organized around business concepts such as products, categories, geographies, customers and time periods. Users expect to view this data from different perspectives— sales by product by week, sales by region by month, etc.— and expect to switch interactively among these perspectives. Users need to see information at different levels of detail, looking for insights with summary data (e.g., sales by category by week), then drilling down to increasing levels of detail (e.g., sales by product by store by day), in order to understand root causes and anomalies.

The term on-line analytical processing, or OLAP, is increasingly used to describe these dimensional applications. In an open client/server environment, two general approaches have emerged to meet this dimensional analysis or OLAP requirement: self-contained multi-dimensional database (MDDBMS) systems, and dimension analysis tools layered directly on a relational database. Both approaches require seamless integration between the tool and the data warehouse.

MDDBMS systems contain only summarized and highly-summarized data, but provide very high performance and rich tools for exploring this data through pivoting, analytic computations, etc. However, when the MDDBMS user needs to "drill down" to greater levels of detail, the user must "escape" from the MDDBMS and directly query the detailed data in the data warehouse. Some MDDBMS products provide such a "drill-through port" to generate and submit SQL queries to a data warehouse, and present the results within the MDDBMS interface.

Effective integration between an MDDBMS and a data warehouse relational database requires the RDBMS natively to support the concept of dimensionality. That is, the same dimensional organization used within the MDDBMS must be available in the RDBMS schema. Otherwise, the detail data in the RDBMS does not correspond to the summary data in the MDDBMS and cannot "roll up" to match the summary data. Equally important, the data warehouse RDBMS must match the performance of the MDDBMS so that when the analyst drills into detail data, the continuity of analysis is maintained.

Seamless dimensional integration is even more critical when dimensional analysis and OLAP tools are layered directly upon a relational database, because in this environment all interactive queries against both summary and detail data must be answered by the RDBMS. The RDBMS must support fast and easy creation and maintenance of pre-computed summaries, must support dynamic calculation of other summaries, and must support detailed data all within one schema design. Interactive performance must be maintained at all levels of summarization.

10. Advanced Query Functionality

SQL, the query language of data warehouses, is powerful and flexible. It allows users to express rich and complex requests for the data they need including sorting, summarization and mathematical calculations. SQL is powerful because it expresses operations in terms of "what" rather than "how." This frees the database server to employ internal algorithms to speed query response while the user is unaware of the internal execution strategy employed by the RDBMS. SQL's value is further increased through standardization, allowing products from different vendors to compete on features and performance.

Despite these strengths, SQL is a remarkably deficient language for expressing and conducting advanced business analysis. Standard SQL is a set-oriented language. This means all operations are defined to operate on unordered data, or more precisely, on indeterminately ordered data. Final results can be sorted, but in standard SQL sorting can only take place after all other processing is complete. This restriction is part of the "what rather than how" design of the SQL language, but it unfortunately precludes standard SQL from answering many useful business questions.

For example, a common operation used in business analysis is moving average. Moving average is used to smooth variability in the source data especially when looking for trends or analyzing changes in the business over time. Unlike computation of a simple average, computation of a moving average depends on the ordering of the data being averaged and thus is an order-dependent operation prohibited by standard SQL.

This conflict between the SQL standard and the business analyst's needs occurs repeatedly in data warehousing. Other examples include the computation of rankings, n-tile orderings, etc. Apart from order-dependent operations, standard SQL also does not include critical statistical operations such as variance and standard deviation.

These deficiencies in SQL push the problem of advanced analysis onto the client workstation, where in order to produce the desired answer, the entire database result set needs to be reprocessed using a spreadsheet, statistical tool or a custom program. This two-step process drastically slows effective query performance, requires the use of several dissimilar tools and significantly increases network capacity requirements because large volumes of raw data are sent to the client workstation for reprocessing.

An effective data warehouse server requires a complete set of business analytic operations to answer the important questions posed by real analysts. Required analytic operations include the core sequential and statistical operations described above, as well as the data type-specific and business domain-specific operations needed to provide all of the answers sought from the data warehouse.

Of course, SQL standardization remains important for application portability and basic interoperability between client tools and the RDBMS server. All credible warehouse RDBMS systems must offer full standard SQL and must process standard SQL with full performance and without other compromise.

Conclusion

We have shown in this white paper that the single most important component of a data warehouse is the RDBMS used to store vast quantities of data and to quickly and reliably answer a wide range of business questions.

Just as on-line transaction processing (OLTP) environments require specialized technologies to satisfy application demands, data warehouse environments require equally specialized technologies.

The requirements for data warehouse RDBMSs begin with the loading and preparation of data for query and analysis. If a product fails to meet the criteria at this stage, the rest of the system will be inaccurate, unreliable and unavailable.

While loading and preparation are necessary steps, they are not sufficient. Query throughput is the measure of success for a data warehouse application. As more questions are answered, analysts are catalyzed to ask more creative and insightful questions.

The most visible and measurable value of implementing a data warehouse is evidenced in the uninhibited, creative access to data it provides the end user.

A data warehouse RDBMS server must fulfill these ten requirements to provide the specialized performance and functionality of today's data warehouse applications.

Notes

Chapter 7

Bringing Performance to Your Data Warehouse

—Lois Richards,
Data Warehousing Product Manager,
Dynamic Information Systems Corporation

Introduction

Organizations continue to compile database structures containing MOUNTAINS of data! More and more users are demanding to have greater and greater access to this data analyzing historical data and finding trends in order to turn this data into viable information. Access to this data is increasingly critical to the competitive advantage and success of every organization. The more historical data an organization maintains, the more valuable that data becomes.

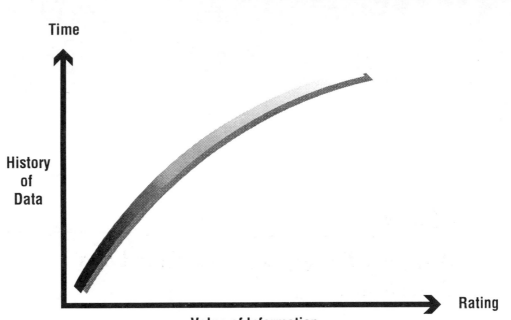

The data warehouse was introduced to provide an accessible storehouse for these volumes of data. The challenge for Information Systems is in bringing a usable, responsive data warehouse application to the user. Building a decision support system around a data warehouse will take Information Systems (IS) into a frontier of new technologies, new terminologies and new concepts. What is not new is the need to plan, design and maintain what is implemented. What also is not new is the large investment in dollars, time and human effort.

With this new environment comes new products touting many claims. IS can provide users with fancy front-end tools to access all the data in the data warehouse. The question then becomes: will the users be able to access the data efficiently and easily, without bringing the system to its knees? Will the ability to wade through mountains of data be better than what users had before? Or will it take hours or days? Will an on-line query be more efficient than submitting the request in batch?

The legacy systems, though they were the source of much of the data, hindered knowledge workers from freely accessing the data for analysis. Their users were subjected to requesting access to this data during low compute demand periods, or even worse in batch or off-line. Thus the data warehouse became the heart of decision support systems to provide on-line analysis of this great history of information.

One obvious requirement of Information Systems is to deliver a data warehouse environment that provides instant access to data. Everywhere, everyone is asking for instant gratification. Instant does not only apply to coffee, microwave meals, or instant relief from aches and pains. Users insist on getting the data they want immediately, or would it be more accurate to say... *yesterday*! The value of the data warehouse translates to locating the data needed, when it is needed.

A good data warehouse will...
> provide the RIGHT data...
>> to the RIGHT people...
>>> at the RIGHT time:
>>>> RIGHT NOW!

This paper looks at the data warehouse architecture and the issues of building a truly responsive decision support environment. It also discusses the technologies that are striving to meet the performance challenge of instant access to data. It will explore some of the options for providing optimum performance in the data warehousing environment. Special focus is paid to the use of Advanced Indexing to bring a truly interactive application to the user. The topics covered are:

- The performance issues for data warehousing

- The methods proposed to address performance

- Types of indexing available

- Using Advanced Indexing to improve performance

- Evaluating an Advanced Indexing technology

The Data Warehouse

Whether you heard it from the source, W. H. Inmon, the *father* of data warehousing, or other authorities in the industry, the definition of a data warehouse is a collection of non-volatile, subject-oriented, time variant, integrated data, stored and maintained for the decision support efforts within an organization. Data warehousing is the blending of various technologies to provide users with information at their fingertips. These technologies assist users in turning data into useful information. The challenge to IS is in integrating these technologies to present users with an efficient, accessible, useable system.

The data warehouse is the hub for decision support data. What is stored in the data warehouse is determined by the user population. When designing a data warehouse, you must consider what data users will need from the legacy systems. You must also take into account the degree of granularity to maintain in the data warehouse whether to store great levels of detail or whether to summarize the data by predetermined requirements. The data warehouse may actually have several levels of detail. Because of the large volumes of data, IS is often concerned not only about the storage of the data, but more so about the ability to provide access to the data without adversely affecting the performance of the system. This is why data archiving was done on legacy systems...

Data archiving was the precursor to the data warehouse. As legacy systems grew, the magnitude of data being stored grew. To reduce the amount of data that users had to sift through, so as to maintain the peak level of performance in legacy applications, historical data was often archived. Unfortunately, data archiving typically meant data was placed off-line, with access limited to pre-arranged batch processing, or even worse, poring over hard-copy reports or print-outs that were generated when the data had been on-line.

User Requirements

Today, users want, and need, on-line access to these large amounts of historical data to do various analysis. And remember, they want that data now! Understanding past trends can help an organization plan for the future. Evaluating the buying trends of customers can assist a marketing department's sales strategy. Assessing a product's historical performance can provide valuable insight into the maintenance of inventory, the introduction of new products, or the retirement of older products. These are just a few of the ways a data warehouse can contribute to an organization's decision making process.

To provide a system to meet the organization's decision support needs, Information Systems must work closely with the end users to understand their data and reporting needs. Even after building the data warehouse with the data required, IS must continue to work with the users to address frequently changing needs. This is because the process of analyzing data and turning it into information requires a dynamically changing environment. Analysis beget more analysis, which beget even more analysis... and on and on! As the user learns more from the data, the information gleaned will prompt more questions and conclusions, as well as new requirements. IS must design a system that will lend itself to this ever-changing environment.

Performance is one area that will need to be continually addressed. An organization's growing history of data must be readily available, on-line. The flow of data from the data warehouse to the user must not be hindered by a system that cannot easily and quickly perform queries to the data.

The Flow of Data

If we look at the data warehousing environment, we see that information flows as represented in the following diagram.

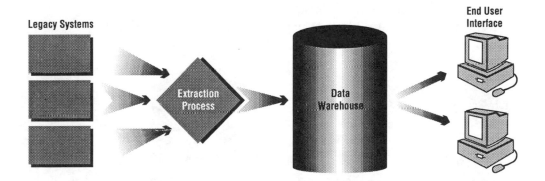

Information flows out of the legacy systems into the data warehouse. The data from legacy systems may be merely loaded into the data warehouse, or the data may actually be massaged or scrubbed before it enters the data warehouse. Once the data warehouse is built, the users can begin to access the information for analysis and the retrieval of data.

Granted, there are other components of the data warehouse (such as metadata, security and warehouse management), but for our purpose, this paper will deal with the basic 4 components: the legacy systems, extraction, the data warehouse, the front-end access.

We must now consider how freely information flows through the data warehouse environment. *Freely* refers to the users' access to data, not from a security standpoint, but more from the ability to find and use data for decision support. Is the data truly accessible and available, or are there bottlenecks?

Performance Issues

Indeed there are bottlenecks. Bottlenecks between the legacy systems and the data warehouse may be a result of volume or coordination of the data. As the data flows out of the legacy systems, there may be issues of synchroniza-tion. As we build our subject-oriented data warehouse, one system may lag behind another in delivering related data. Once the data is loaded into the data warehouse, we are then faced with a possible retrieval bottleneck. *Data warehouse*, by virtue of the definition, implies BIG databases. Each knowledge worker must read through all this data to extract the information needed. All this processing of the data in the data warehouse will certainly impact performance and cause bottlenecks for the decision support application.

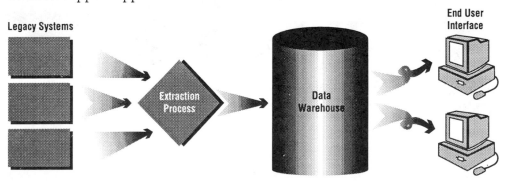

Let's consider these retrieval bottlenecks. What could be contributing to them? There is really only one possibility: *too much data is being processed!* Data warehouses adversely impact I/O processing. The access of these large amounts of data can slow down any transfer of data from the disk drive to the processor. This is because the processor is forced to read through all the data in order to process the users' queries. Networks will also experience the effects of large volumes of data being moved to users' PCs. In this case, users may unnecessarily transfer large amounts of data down to their PCs for analysis.

Even if users require less data than expected, they can still affect the system performance by entering an erroneous request. That request may again cause too much data to be processed! Even worse, if the user gets the wrong information, the user may actually make the request again. In an attempt to correct the problem, the user may think that the next request will be the right one. This is magnified when applications are too complicated for the average user to understand. Needless to say, valuable processing time is being used to retrieve, or sometimes just read through, volumes of wrong information.

Ideally, we should allow the users to consider their requests, whether by taking various slices of the data, or by starting with a large view of the data and then whittling it down to smaller amounts of data. Users should not have to worry that the requests they make may adversely impact performance! Also, we should not waste the users' time. Knowledge workers should not have to wait hours for the results, or work late when the system is least busy. It becomes imperative that we address the performance bottlenecks before the data warehouse is built!

Addressing Bottlenecks

There are various options being proposed in the data warehouse environment to address performance bottlenecks. Some are new technologies. Others have been around for some time. They are:

- Parallel processing (MPP)

- Multidimensional servers

- Distributed warehouse

- OLAP (or multidimensional queries)

- Data marts

- Partitioning

- Query regulation/police

- Advanced Indexing: inverted indexes, bit-map indexes

We can categorize these technologies into two areas: those that impact the hardware environment and those that impact the software environment. In hardware, there is massively parallel process (MPP), dedicated multidimen-sional servers and distributing the warehouse across processors. In software, there is OLAP, partitioning the data warehouse, distributing portions of the data warehouse to application specific needs (data marts), query regulation and indexing.

As we examine these options, two parties must always be considered: the user group, and the Information Systems group. Any solution must benefit both groups. Too often, a solution benefits one group while the other group suffers. The knowledge workers may not get the system they need to do their jobs. The IS group may become burdened with a solution that is cumbersome and expensive to maintain. This in turn can cause requests for additional solutions, and the users to suffer. As we discuss each option, we will keep this in mind and note whenever an option could present a *win-win* solution for both groups.

The Hardware Approach

If we first consider the hardware approaches, we see technology moving toward faster processing and bigger data storage capabilities. The computer industry has always been able to build a better chip that will process data faster. The industry has also been able to build on-line storage devices that can hold massive amounts of information. These advances allow us to process more data faster. If the system starts to run slow, buy a faster processor. If we need to store more data, purchase a bigger storage drive. This may appear to be a simple solution to our performance problem. The drawbacks are that this may be a very expensive solution and it may provide a quick, but only temporary fix. This is partially because the connection between the fast processor and the big drive has not made proportionally the same advances.

What seems to be lagging is the ability to build a *pipeline* that effectively moves all that data between the fast processor and the huge data storage device. Whether the *pipeline* is direct to the CPU or over a network, the movement of data from storage to CPU has continued to constrain the system from performing at its peak. We continue to hear warnings in the data warehouse arena to make sure we *manage* the network now that data warehousing is introducing such volumes of data movement across systems. So how will a faster processor address the management of massive amounts of data if there are still issues about getting the data to and from the processor? It cannot, without help.

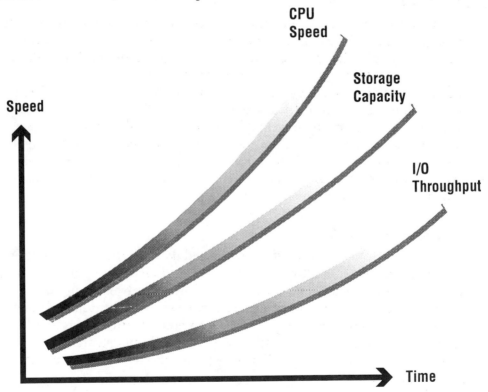

Parallel Processing

One proposal is to give the processor some more processors to help do the work. Parallel processing divides the work among multiple processors. This requires that the relational database management system be able to divide its work among these processors. Therefore one processor could scan the database, while another could sort data, while another could perform a table join. If this is not a feature of the relational database, parallel processing becomes a task of IS, where IS must programmatically *funnel* each task to a processor. If you have been in the industry for any length of time, you may recognize this as throwing more hardware at the problem. It aids in relieving performance bottlenecks, but does not provide a permanent solution to the I/O bottleneck.

A way of thinking about parallel processing is to compare it to handling rush hour traffic. If we have a million cars coming into the city every morning, would it be better to add more roads (or lanes on the highway), or would it be better to lessen the number of cars coming into the city? If more people car-pooled or took public transportation, there would be less cars on the roads. This is the concept behind parallel processing (more lanes) versus indexing (less cars traveling the same roads). With parallel processing, users may see an immediate improvement in performance, but the tendency is for the performance to flatten, then deteriorate. As users experience a performance degradation, this is an indication that a processor needs to be added, putting IS in a constant react mode.

Multidimensional Servers

Another option is to create a specialized database that will maintain the data in a format geared toward the type of retrievals users will be making. These multidimensional databases require investment in proprietary databases and are often placed on a dedicated server. Multidimensional servers require new design approaches, consequently impacting the IS maintenance load and costs. Using relational technology, standard RDBMSs, eases maintenance issues— both resource maintenance and administration.

Distributed Data Warehouse

Distributing the data warehouse takes a similar approach to parallel processing. Divide the data warehouse into data subsets and place each on a separate processor unit. We again distribute the workload. Like parallel processing, this can become a maintenance nightmare for IS.

The Software Approach

With the software approach we address the performance dilemma from the standpoint of the user. What if we could control the types of queries the user will do?

OLAP

OLAP (on-line analytical processing), or multidimensional querying, tunes the system for analysis, much like the OLTP approach which tunes performance around the transaction. OLAP (or multidimensional querying) takes the approach of defining the *dimensions* that the knowledge worker will require. OLAP claims to support complex queries, but appears to lend itself more to a *predictive* analysis of the data warehouse. True ad-hoc querying may be limited.

Data Marts

Another form of distributing the data creates *mini* data warehouses (data marts). Data marts also address specific decision support application needs. These subsets of the data warehouse can be on one or multiple hardware platforms. Distributing the data can become a burden for IS. If you consider the dynamic nature of decision support systems— an application that changes often— then any environment that requires a continual assessment of design, location and access of the data can become a major undertaking to maintain. Similar to the *islands of automation*, data marts can lead to *islands of data warehouses*, where IS will need to build bridges between data marts.

Partitioning

Partitioning improves the retrieval performance by segmenting the data into logical areas. A good example of this is if you were to automate all the phone books in the country. Very likely, the letter *S* may be about 25 - 35% of all the names. This is based on the assumption that *Smith* is the most common English surname. You could partition your data so that all surnames starting with *S* are on their own partition. Therefore, when you need to look up a name beginning with *S*, you would only look at the one set of data. Also, when you look up any surnames beginning with letters other than *S*, you would not have to read through the *S* data.

The downside to partitioning is that it requires constant tuning in a dynamic environment where unpredictable queries are made. A query this week may look at one partition, but next week the same users queries may span two or more partitions. This could conceivably become a warehouse management nightmare for IS, as well as delay users needs for ad-hoc queries.

Query Regulation

With query regulation, we now *manage* the user's side of the decision support application. This method encompasses *trapping* the user's query, assessing the query and then determining if, when and how the query will be performed. This option is not totally transparent to the user (especially if it is determined that the query will not be performed, or will be performed at a later time). This could not only be a full-time support issue for IS, but query regulation could also adversely affect the knowledge worker's ability to freely access the data warehouse.

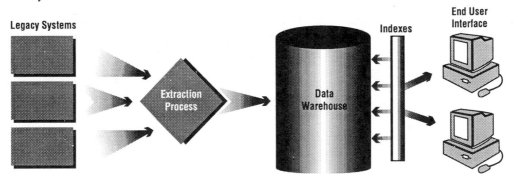

Advanced Indexing

Our final approach to address performance bottlenecks is the use of Advanced Indexing— different from traditional indexing. Advanced Indexing augments relational and flat file structures by providing access functions above and beyond the native index. If we consider first the characteristics of a data warehouse/decision support system, we'll be able to isolate how Advanced Indexing can improve performance in many areas.

Data warehousing records the history of an organization. Decision support spots trends and locates strengths and weaknesses in the organization. From the knowledge workers standpoint, the decision support system must provide the ability to query the organizational data warehouse in various ways. These query needs can be categorized as follows:

- Ad hoc querying

- Support for complex queries (multidimensional "slice and dice")

- Drill-downs through data

- Quantity qualified (counts)

- Summary calculations (sum, average, maximum, minimum)

In the area of moving the data from raw form to true information, the knowledge worker must be able to *communicate* the data to others in the organizations. This now places presentation requirements on the system that include listings of results (display detail), graphical display of the results, cross tabulations and summarization display (totals, averages and other aggregations).

Client/Server applications provide the state-of-the art access to data from the PC. Knowledge workers can download data to their favorite PC tool and analyze to their hearts content. Prior to PC networks, users had to copy data down to their PC (via PC copy tools or re-keying). This also required the users' understanding of the data on the server or IS's intervention in extracting data for the PC users. Client/server applications automated this process.

Unfortunately, client/server introduced some special issues. Client/server applications allowed users to request data from the host system. If the users was granted access to the data, it was theirs for the taking. So the PC user could ask for *all of last month's sales for their specific region.* This may have only qualified 5,000 records out of a 10 million record data warehouse. What was not evident to the user was the database access method (a complex SQL statement that likely generated several slow serial reads of the database) as well as the impact on the network in transferring these 5,000 records. All the user knew was that the client/server application made it so much more easier to request the data needed, and that sometimes it took hours to complete the request. Every now and then, the user would also be asked to perform the queries at night, or on the weekends.

The problems and issues faced by the data warehouse/decision support system is the inability to query efficiently (query optimizers), limitations on performing complex queries (query police) and overall poor performance (serial searches). We must either ask the knowledge workers to cautiously use the computer resources (no runaway queries), or ask IS to continually *police* the system (prevent runaway queries). This of course hinders the knowledge worker from trying various queries (Will this cause a runaway query and will IS ban me from ever using the system on-line again???). It also hinders IS from bringing new or enhanced systems on-line (Will I have to spend more time making sure that the system is not running at snail's pace because of a poorly structured SQL query, or will I ever have any time to add new capabilities??)

So, again our goal is to allow the users to peruse the data freely, without asking them to worry about the requests they are making and without adversely impacting performance! And just as importantly: without asking them to wait hours for the results, or work late when the system is least busy. Additionally, we want to give IS the ability to provide these services without asking them to maintain the system while sacrificing the ability to provide new services to the users.

How can Advanced Indexing help performance?

Yes, indexing is a concept familiar to database managers and administrators, yet it is a technology that has been enhanced to go way beyond its original use. So often we look at indexing as the traditional indexes that come with the database or file system. Indexing originally provided a pointer to data, allowing for greater efficiency in accessing data. Like an index in a book, the index provides you with the direct address of the information needed. Without the index, you would have to read every page in the book to find the subject you seek. Tried and true, the index always assured a fast retrieval of data. Unfortunately, the index fell into disrepute! Indexes were relegated to being numeric codes, rarely a few digits and easily forgotten computer ids. Indexes also placed limits on how the user could ask for the information. If you didn't know the *code* to locate the data, you couldn't get to the data. Even if you were then allowed to use some more familiar data (such as name or location or description), you would be required to enter this data exactly the way it was originally entered into the database.

Looking at it from the day to day use, a customer had to know their customer code or vendor code or product code in order to have access to their record of information seemingly *locked away* in the computer. Heaven forbid that you would be allowed to look up anything by your name or company name or address or product description! That would probably take hours, possibly days!!! Why was this?

Let's consider the basic premise of computers. These machines do what they are told; information is processed in a linear manner. Instruction A is executed, then B, then C and so forth. Humans can process instruction B, then C, then A, in whatever order desired. The difference is computers process instructions faster! Where humans can look at a set of instructions and assess if all need to be done, the computer still has not reached that level of sophistication. So why not help the computer! Have it process less instructions. This is the idea behind indexing.

What would happen if we didn't have an index? Just like the example of trying to find a subject in a book, the computer will start at the beginning and read every word to find the subject requested, unlike the non-silicon based unit who would flip through the pages and scan the book first. Computers, however, could perform the task faster than the human. But let's say we give the computer an index to read that will point to the data needed. By giving the computer less to read (based on the fact that the index is an *abbreviated* view of the information contained in the full text), you allow the computer to more efficiently work.

Indexing allows users to find what they need with as few disk I/O's as possible. From **Using the Data Warehouse**, W. H. Inmon says, "The first step the end user can take toward good performance is to use indexes when accessing data. Using an index allows for only selected records to be accessed rather than for the access of massive amounts of records, most of which are not needed. This simple measure is quite effective and can cut down resource utilization enormously in the processing of a query." Allowing the user to localize the data needed without looking through all the data will certainly improve the efficiency and performance of the application.

Another option is to let the index do all the work whenever possible. This is often seen when users would like just a tally of records or an aggregation of specific data items. In **Building the Data Warehouse**, W. H. Inmon says, "A fairly standard database management system feature is that of being able to do index-only processing. On many occasions it is possible to service a request by simply looking in an index (or indexes). When a request can be satisfied by looking only at indexes, it is much more efficient not to have to go to the primary source of data. But not all DBMS are intelligent enough to know that a request can be satisfied in the index." The issue here is to find the indexing product that can efficiently provide fast access to data.

In a data warehouse environment, allowing the computer to more efficiently access and retrieve data becomes more imperative. The volumes of data in the data warehouse far exceed the data found in traditional legacy systems. Advanced Indexing improves performance several ways: better memory utilization, improved disk I/O, alleviate network traffic. Advanced Indexing can exploit the CPU, memory and network performance.

So in summary, an Advanced Index technology that can:

- speed retrieval access,

- enhance function,

- index multiple database platforms, and

- efficiently store indexes,

will truly bring value to any data warehouse solution. Industry experts have long touted the innumerable ways that an index can be used effectively.

Indexing Options

Before looking at your indexing options, we must first discuss the two ways to access data: non-keyed access and keyed access. Non-keyed access uses no index. Each record of the database is accessed sequentially, beginning with the first record, then second, third and so on. This access is good when you wish to access a large portion of the database (greater than 85%). Keyed access provides direct addressing of records. A unique number or character(s) is used to locate and access records. In this case, when specified records are required (say, record 120, 130, 200 and 500), indexing is much more efficient than reading all the records in between.

Indexing comes in various flavors. There are indexes native to the relational database structure: primary indexes, B-tree indexes and hashed/hashing indexes. There are also specialized indexes, independent of the relational database structure: inverted indexes and bit-map indexes. We have referred to these specialized indexes as Advanced Indexing. Advanced Indexing provides the efficiency of indexing (fast access) with additional functionality. We will examine each.

Relational databases come with native indexing capabilities. When developing a relational database structure, database administrators (DBAs) may assign unique numeric data items called primary keys. When you know a record's unique identifier, using the primary key will be the fastest method of retrieving that record. Entering the primary key requires that you know the full value input for the best performance.

The most common indexing method is the B-tree, a method of organizing database keys for searches. B-tree indexes maintain a list of primary keys. You can search through the B-tree to locate the record you are looking for without having to search through the database. Consequently, less data is read, and the computer can efficiently find the full record of data using the key. B-tree indexing provides full and partial key retrievals, sorted key retrievals and concatenation of columns. With B-tree indexes you effectively get single key access to data where rows (or records) are located based on left justification and case sensitive matching.

B-trees are great when you know exactly what you are going after. Unfortunately, decision support implies that we are looking for certain trends or generalities about the data in the data warehouse. What products were the best sellers during the first six months of the year? Who are the top 10 customers? What vendors in the Eastern region give the highest markup? These questions look at the complete data warehouse and then extract data based on the records meeting the criteria. We may have no idea which records will qualify. In fact, the answers to such questions may change over time.

Another similar indexing technique is hashing or hashed indexes. In this indexing technique, an algorithm is used to *calculate* the location of a record. Hashing also requires a full key value lookup and an exact match, including upper and lower case letters, spaces and punctuation. Like B-trees, hashing is limited in delivering the ad-hoc requirements of a data warehouse environment.

So how can we take advantage of the efficiency of direct accessing of data through indexes, and overcome the limitations placed on using B-tree or hashed indexing? The answer is to use inverted indexes. Inverted indexes store the pointers to a database as data and the data from the database as keys. Inverted indexes expedite fast, ad-hoc searches of previously undefined queries. If a table contains sales data with records 1, 5, 13, 22 and 70 representing the WESTERN region, an inverted index would contain WESTERN with pointers to records 1, 5, 13, 22 and 70.

Inverted indexes are ideal for data warehouse applications. This indexing technique lends itself to true ad-hoc querying where the knowledge worker can search for data based on the content, as opposed to designated computer ids. Now the user can enter product description instead of product code, customer name instead of customer number, or region name instead of region id. Additionally, users are not constrained to know exactly how the text was entered. Was that 'John J. Smith', or 'Smith, John J.' or 'SMYTH, Jon J.'? An inverted index can look for any record in the CUSTOMER NAME column that contains the words that sound like 'John' or 'Smith', whether they were entered in all upper case or not!

Benefits to the data warehouse

Indexing is efficient because it directly accesses records, delivering lower I/O's to the database. Benchmarks using Advanced Indexing inverted indexes have demonstrated performance improvements of up to 1000%. Advanced Indexing can protect your investments in existing systems because it requires no special hardware or major restructure of the relational database. Advanced Indexing allows you to ramp-up your applications, that is, build or add as you go. Compared to the other options, Advanced Indexing requires less maintenance and can be less costly overall.

Benchmarks have indicated that inverted indexes can improve retrieval speeds phenomenally. Tests were performed against various data file structures, including relational and flat file. A query performed on a 1 million record database needed to find all customers in Texas who ordered last month. This required a cross table join, based on a free-format address field in the CUSTOMER file and a date range in the ORDER file.

The results were astounding:

	Without Inverted Indexes	With Inverted Indexes
Oracle	33 minutes	1.6 seconds
Rdb	36 minutes	1.7 seconds
Digital RMS	42 minutes	2.5 seconds

By simply placing inverted indexes on columns that you know many users will query, IS is assured the optimum performance in data access. So not only do users have more flexibility in the types of queries they can perform and the speed they perform, but IS also benefits because there is no special hardware or high maintenance issues associated with inverted indexes.

One unique benefit to the data warehouse affects granularity. Granularity impacts the amount of detail kept in the warehouse. The more granular the data, the more detail stored. Inverted indexing supports the storage of lots of detail. With an inverted indexing technology, the requirement to aggregate data into summarization tables saves many hours of file design and maintenance for IS. Index-only summarization capabilities are available today with inverted indexing.

Inverted Indexes are also well suited for applications that include external data sources. So often the case with external data sources is that you have little or no control of the format of the data. This may require extensive resources to *restructure* the data into the organization's standards. One example is of an information provider who loaded data that exceeded the limits of the file structure in place. The existing file structure could not index one particular column which contained greater than 250 character data. Unfortunately, this column of data was the main item the users desired to query the file with. Could this organization allow users to perform a serial read of a 18 GB table for every request? Inverted Indexes came to their rescue! By implementing an inverted indexing technology, this organization was able to supply their users with instant access to the records needed without requiring either the IS development staff or the user to jump through hoops.

Another specialized indexing technology is bit-map indexing. Bit map indexing takes the underlying file structure and for each unique value, represents the data as an array of bits that are then set ON or OFF. For low cardinality data (few unique values such as Male/Female, Yes/No, coded data), bit-map indexing is ideal. Its weakness however is in high cardinality data (many varying values such as text data, name and descriptive fields). Also, although bit-mapped indexing can address the need to do index-only process, many bit-mapped indexes force you to index the whole structure, conse-quently duplicating the data warehouse. Even though some products say "archive the data warehouse and deal only with the index," you then pay the price for the additional processes needed to convert back to the raw data.

Conclusion

So in conclusion, consider a tried and true option. In such an emerging technology as data warehousing, where every week there is a new product or component being introduced, proven and demonstrable results are imperative. Do you want to be put in a position of trying a *bleeding edge* technology to build your corporation's future direction on? With advance indexing technologies, you can more easily bring in new technologies for testing while you still have a functioning, responsive system. Better yet, wait until these new technologies have gotten the *kinks* out.

BOTTOM LINE: Advanced Indexing can leverage investments in existing hardware and software, integrating in new technologies while protecting much of the application developed. Inverted Indexes provide the broadest range of flexibility for decision support/data warehouse applications.

Chapter 8

Targeted Marketing and the Data Warehouse

—Red Brick Systems

Introduction

Data warehousing is emerging as the cornerstone of a new category of applications targeted to help organizations retain, grow, satisfy, and get the most from their customers in ways never before possible.

With these new "customer intimacy" applications, organizations want to:

1. Get closer to customers to better understand their needs quicker;
2. Learn from past experience to predict their customers' future behavior; and,
3. Target customers with the highest potential to maximize revenue and return on investment.

Up to now, data warehouse applications have been successful at improving business performance through applications such as logistics and distribution analysis, trend analysis, budget analysis, category management and claims analysis. The common element in these applications is the use of "business facts" such as products sold, price paid, promotions and seasonality for analysis.

The most important element in the new breed of customer-centric data warehouse applications is the invaluable information asset that businesses have accumulated about their customers.

Applications to improve profitability and grow revenues through a better understanding of customer needs reach across all industries, including retail, telecommunications, hospitality, retail banking, credit card providers, transportation, and consumer products. These applications include customer profiling, customer retention analysis, customer profitability analysis, campaign planning, micro-marketing and cross-product holding analysis.

Businesses also face challenges such as integrating and managing customer information to improve marketing and service, equipping front-line personnel to market products and services more effectively and identifying cross-selling opportunities.

Studies have shown that an increase in customer retention of only two percent had the same profit impact as a 10 percent reduction in operating costs. Moreover, it can cost five times more to acquire a new customer than to retain an existing one. Other studies have shown that businesses typically derive 80 percent of their business from existing customers yet spend only 20 percent of their resources on them. Conversely, these same businesses expend 80 percent of their business development effort and resources on obtaining new customers which produce only 20 percent of their business.

Corporate thirst for creative insight, coupled with an ever-increasing desire to understand each individual customer, has led to a new type of analysis for customer-centric data warehouse applications.

Database marketing is a classic example of this type of analysis. Analysts look for that "market of one" segmentation to better target specific products or services to specific consumers. By drilling down within the customer table, much richer insight can be harvested to help predict buyer habits.

New data warehousing technologies help analysts search deeper into corporate data and enable these exciting new applications to become a critical factor in more organizations.

Open, relational data warehouse servers are the right model for supporting these new customer-centric applications. The demands for scale, number of users, and analytic functions far exceed the capabilities of so-called "universal servers." To meet these requirements effectively, an open RDBMS architected from the ground up for these applications is mandatory.

Using a Data Warehouse for Customer Analysis

It is generally accepted that the most effective model for a data warehouse is what is called a "STAR" schema. STAR designs provide an intuitive representation of data which is conducive to analyst exploration and, when used with STARjoin processing capability, offer the best performance for complex query processing.

In the early days of data warehouse development, STAR models appeared to be very simplistic, containing factual information in one table, and qualitative data in other, smaller tables which surrounded the facts and defined business "dimensions." These dimensions might be factors such as time period, geography, product or customer.

Today, data warehouse models have evolved to robust "galaxies" of interconnected STAR schemas with multiple tables of factual data and numerous dimension tables linked to secondary dimensions, roll-up data, and other galaxies. What results is a database nightmare where even the simplest of business questions results in 10-way joins processing hundreds of millions of records at a time.

Another key trend in data warehouse architectures is the creation of very large dimension tables characterized by larger cardinalities and wider rows of multiple attributes. An example of this is today's "customer" dimension.

Customer data is the single most important information asset in micro-marketing and presents a unique challenge to the data warehouse architecture. In this day of "lists," it is common to see customer tables with cardinalities in the millions if not the tens of millions of rows.

An additional complication is that each row in the "general" customer table may consist of multiple low-selectivity attributes like gender, age group, ethnic group, zip code, income category, educational level, etc. For example, if one were to select all male customers, roughly half the number of rows from the customer table would qualify. While this is an expected outcome for such a query, it highlights several difficulties for traditional database management systems.

Indexing Strategies

Most important among these is the indexing strategy (access technology) used by most general RDBMSs. B-tree indexing is the core access technology for most RDBMSs. Using a standard B-tree index for attributes of low-selectivity is inherently inefficient. This inefficiency results from the fact that B-trees are generally designed for reasonably selective columns (typically five percent or less).

In addition, B-tree indexes are typically built for a single-column, highly-selective constraint evaluation. So, if a query is looking for men who are age 35, have a high income, play golf, and are white-collar professionals, it's possible that five separate B-tree indexes would have to be consulted to find all qualifying records.

For the purpose of illustration, let's review a customer table with 10 million records. Consider the following query:

```
SELECT count(customer_id)
FROM customer_table WHERE
gender = male AND
income_category = HIGH AND
education_level = MASTERS
AND zip_code = 95032;
```

Traditional RDBMS engines will optimize this query and produce one of two strategies for execution.

Alternative 1

- Evaluate the most selective constraint,
- Generate a list of rows that qualify, and
- Evaluate the remaining constraints for each of the rows generated above which will produce the answer to the query.

This method retrieves rows based on the most selective constraint using only the index for that column, followed by a sequential evaluation of each of the other constraints in a post-retrieval manner. Thus, if `education_level` is deemed most selective, all rows that match the `education_level` constraint are retrieved followed by a successive row-by-row constraint evaluation; i.e., that of `gender`, `income_category`, and `zip_code`.

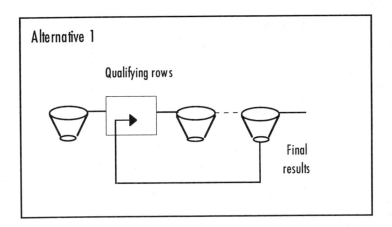

This method is extremely expensive from an I/O standpoint. This is because of the large number of rows that qualify from the first step by virtue of the low selectivity of the attribute. For example, if there are four unique education levels and we assume an even distribution, then each education level would produce 2.5 million qualifying records from a 10 million row customer table.

Furthermore, the execution plan does not take advantage of any indexes created on the less selective attributes, resulting in a considerable space overhead with minimal return.

Alternative 2

A somewhat more advanced approach which is not quite as resource-intensive as Alternative 1 consists of the following steps:

- evaluate each constraint by using a different B-tree index on each attribute, which results in a list of rows that qualify for each of the constraints,

- merge the lists successively to form one master list that satisfies all the constraints, and,

- retrieve the qualifying rows to produce the answer to the query.

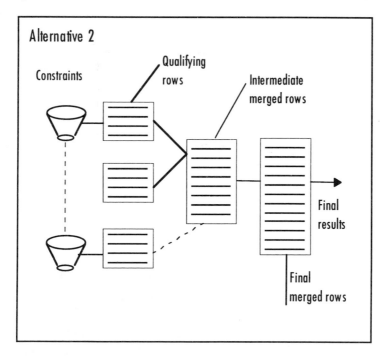

Though this may seem like a fairly trivial task, it is still CPU and I/O intensive. I/O is heavy because the selectivity of each of the attributes is low, and the number of qualifying records for each attribute is large. Similarly, this alternative is CPU intensive as each of the lists have to be compared and then merged into a master list that satisfies all constraints.

Another issue in this approach is that each of the B-tree indexes is inefficient by virtue of each attribute's low selectivity; that is, each key value will have multiple records which result in inefficient spatial representation in the index.

More Than Just Selecting on Attributes

The query (example 1) represents a very simplistic type of analysis that could be referred to as "selective identification." That is, the query attempts to identify qualifying rows based on several attribute properties. This typically answers the "who and how many" type of business question.

In general, this type of query is not very interesting to a market analyst. More than just wanting to know "who," the analyst will often need a deeper understanding of "who did what." In this case, the "selective identification" query must be followed by a more traditional database join operation to pull in other data elements.

Consider the following modification to the prior query:

```
SELECT customer_id, sum(dollars)
FROM customer_table a,
facts b, products c, time d
WHERE gender = male AND
income_category = HIGH AND
education_level = MASTERS
AND zip_code = 95032 AND
product = "Baseballs" AND
period = "Spring" AND
a.id = b.id AND b.prod = c.prod
AND d.id = b.id;
```

In this query, the database must first identify the customers matching the "selective identification" criteria from the customer table followed by a four-way join among the fact, product, time, and customer tables. This will ultimately produce a list of selected customers and the total dollars they spent on purchases of baseballs in spring.

The important requirement to complete this query is that the database must be able to solve both the *selection* problem as well as the *join* problem. These two aspects need to be integrated seamlessly so that the result of processing the "selective identification" portion of the criteria feeds into the join processing algorithm.

See *Appendix A, Using an Index to Target Customers,* for a discussion of Red Brick's approach to addressing the issues.

Chapter 9

Paradigm Shattered: How the Web Will Redefine the Role of the Data Warehouse

— Michael J. Saylor, President and CEO
MicroStrategy, Inc.

Introduction

The passage of time and the progress of industry consists of long periods of execution, punctuated by intermittent bursts of metamorphosis. We are currently entering one such transitional phase in the information technology industry. The concept of the data warehouse is being redefined by the Internet.

That system of open networking protocols has forever changed the economics of information dissemination, catalyzing an entirely new class of software programs. The result is the commercial decision support application— a concept so simple that a child can understand its significance, so powerful that it will remake entire sectors of our economy forever, and so compelling that every knowledge worker will grow dependent upon at least one of these within the decade.

Data Warehouse as Corporate Memory

The data warehouse, like most successful technological innovations, is the beneficiary of a fortunate change in economic circumstance. Corporations exist to perform transactions, the most significant of these generally being the sale to a customer of either products or services. Having succeeded in performing these transactions, the next great challenge is to optimize the process and innovate new varieties of the offering. Doing this well requires that the company remember the exact details of its business dealings. Unfortunately, for most of human history, the tools for recording and later analysis of transactions have been woefully insufficient.

The status quo at the dawning of the data warehouse era (early '90s) was proprietary hardware and database software from vendors such as IBM, Teradata, and Tandem. The cost to accumulate and analyze 100 gigabytes of data (approximately one year worth of store-item-week information for a typical retail chain) might exceed $25 million. After discounting for the risk of in-house development, delays between project initiation and completion, and the attendant management drain of such a large undertaking, it is easy to see why an experienced executive would be reluctant to go forward with any project that did not promise to deliver a return in excess of $100 million. With an economic hurdle this high, experimentation by IT visionaries was effectively stifled, and large database development remained the province of a few mega-organizations.

All of this changed with the advent of parallel processing hardware running the UNIX operating system, coupled with merchant RDBMS capable of exploiting multiple threads simultaneously for processes such as data loads, indexing, aggregation, cleansing, and queries. UNIX introduced competition for the hardware platform. Merchant RDBMS introduced competition for the software platform. As might be expected, prices plummeted. By early 1994, it was possible to put together an open systems configuration capable of hosting 100 gigabytes of data for a few million dollars, and companies could get started with pilot projects for a fraction of that cost. As conventional economics dictate, when the cost of a commodity decreases by an order of magnitude, demand normally increases even faster— assuming any pent-up demand.

We need not have worried about any lack of demand. Retail, consumer packaged goods, insurance, healthcare, telecommunications, transportation, entertainment, manufacturing, government, and financial services organizations embraced this technology with a vengeance. The justification was generally improvement of operational efficiency in areas such as merchandising, category management, logistics, promotions, marketing and sales programs, asset management, cost containment, pricing, and product development. As of today, data warehouses either exist or are in the process of being created in 90% of the midsize and large corporations in the US. They represent the corporate memory, and grow in both size as well as asset value with every day that passes.

World Wide Web as Information Accelerator

Throughout history, crucial developments in information technology have accelerated the pace of human endeavor. The spoken word made it possible for us to exchange information in small groups at a single point in time. The tribal culture was born. The written word allowed us to *narrowcast* information to those who were far away in either time or space. Distributed government became viable, with the finest example in the western world being the Roman Empire. In the fifteenth century, the invention of the printing press decreased the cost of distributing written information by orders of magnitude, providing an information *broadcast* capability for the first time in human history. What followed was an unprecedented acceleration in rational thought, which we now refer to as the Renaissance. The Scientific Revolution, the Protestant Reformation, European Nationalism, and the Industrial Revolution all trace their roots to Gutenberg's invention, which made economical the dissemination of information critical to their movement. In Thomas Kuhn's (author of The Structure of Scientific Revolutions) parlance, the introduction of the printing press would be referred to as a paradigm shift. Events that took place after its acceptance would be impossible without its existence, and inconceivable before its invention.

The World Wide Web represents a paradigm shift of comparable significance to that of the printing press. Rather than broadcast the written word (static information), the WWW broadcasts entire software applications (dynamic information). Similar to the economic impact of the printing press on text, the web decreases the cost of distributing a given piece of software functionality by orders of magnitude. In order to understand this phenomenon better, let's consider an example:

In anticipation of the approaching demand for housing in Atlanta during the Olympic games, a group of hotel owners joined together to create a program that allows consumers to search for and book appropriate lodging. They deployed this functionality over the web via a site entitled:

http://www.stayinatlanta.com

Assuming that it costs about $250,000 to create the application, and another $750,000 in hardware to meet the likely transaction load each day, we arrive at a total system cost of about $1,000,000. That system would be capable of accepting thousands of requests per day from a pool of 10,000,000+ potential users.

Now, consider the costs to implement the same system via conventional client/server technology. To allow for a pool of even 1,000,000 potential users would require the software developer to ship 2,000,000 floppy disks (assume 2 disks to install the program), utilize 10,000 gigabytes of hard disk space (assume the software requires 10 megabytes of disk space on each user's machine), print and ship 500 tons of software manuals (assume each set of documentation weighs 1 pound), and staff a help desk to spend 330,000 hours on the telephone answering user questions (assuming 1 question per user, which requires 20 minutes of a staffer's time). By the time we total the materials, installation, maintenance, and support costs of this configuration, we can quite easily imagine total expenses to distribute our application in excess of $100,000,000. After adjusting for the marketing necessary to convince 1,000,000 people to install our software on their machines, it becomes clear that without a business case likely to generate hundreds of millions in value added, client/server distribution at this scale doesn't make much sense.

Comparing the web vs. traditional client/server technology, we see that the web offers massive economic advantages for those needing to distribute software broadly. The break-even point for web development is much lower, which naturally results in much greater application diversity. Additionally, the variable costs of web deployment are also lower, meaning that any applications deployed in this environment will have a much higher gross margin (i.e., be more profitable).

As the above example illustrates, the World Wide Web is a superconductor for all those software applications that run effectively through its application programming interface. It plays the same role for software programmers that the printing press played for authors five centuries ago-making it possible for them to project their knowledge throughout the society to an unprecedented degree. Before the printing press, the rich man possessed a few books. Today, it is not uncommon for a member of the middle class to own a hundred books or more, with quick access to hundreds of thousands. Before the web, a professional with a home computer was likely to have access to a half-dozen major computer programs. After the web, that same professional can now access thousands of programs.

Just as thousands of mass-produced books on subjects such as engineering, manufacturing, and navigation became the building blocks for the industrial age, so shall thousands of massively distributed software programs for communication, engineering, and decision making become the building blocks for the coming information age. In an instant, the web has emerged as the low-cost distribution channel for software— in many cases so low that it allows knowledge workers to self-publish their work. The result is a drastic increase in the velocity of information flow. Expertise (in the form of software) emerges, is distributed, tuned, modulated, and amplified with frightening speed over the global Internet. The collective intellect of humanity, which is our fundamental engine of growth, thinks faster and grows wiser.

Two Great Forces Collide

As we have discussed above, the success of the data warehousing movement has resulted in a massive increase in the amount of data being captured for decision support, as well as an increase in the number of decision support applications available. The more recent proliferation of the World Wide Web has provided the world with a revolutionary distribution channel for software programs. The example below serves to illustrate the synergy between the forces of distribution and production:

Imagine you inherit a farm in central Pennsylvania, and by chance discover massive oil deposits underlying your property while digging a well. The year is 1825 and there is not a railroad to be found. How much is this farm worth? Lacking any effective methods to refine this oil into kerosene (for lighting lamps) and transport that kerosene to the eastern markets, the oil would be worthless.

The lack of effective distribution channels and production capabilities for refined oil crippled the industry development for many years. By 1875, with the arrival of the first modern rail transportation systems, the critical distribution bottleneck was broken, and John D. Rockefeller was rapidly building the Standard Oil Company. The distribution leverage provided by those railroads provided the revenues necessary to perfect Standard's refinery technology, and those refineries turned out increasing quantities and varieties of petroleum byproducts. By exploiting those "worthless" oil deposits, Rockefeller soon accumulated more wealth than any person of his generation.

The massive accumulations of commercial data are analogous to the above oil deposits. Hardware, databases, and decision support software constitute the essential technologies for "refining" this raw data. Building a data warehouse is similar to building an oil refinery. The World Wide Web is the transportation system for refined product. The critical shift that occurs at this point is the creation of a merchant decision support business. In other words, with the Internet as a distribution channel, it becomes possible for corporations to utilize their data warehouse as a revenue-generating, rather than cost-reducing, asset.

Consider the opportunities available to a telecommunications company to obtain value from its database of telephone calls. By providing decision support applications over the web against a comprehensive data warehouse containing call-level details for all customers, the telecommunications firm can offer its customers answers to the following types of questions on a continuous basis:

- Which calls are most likely to be fraudulent charges? When and where do they occur?

- How are my calls distributed by employee, location, office, department, time period, etc.?

- How much does it cost me to call each of my customers each month?

- What percentage of the time do my telesales reps spend on the phone? What is the average length of their phone calls? Which prospects do they speak with? How many calls do we spend on average with each prospect?

- Which customers get 80% of my field sales force's calling attention? How much time does the typical field sales rep spend on the phone each month?

- Where do my callers live? How often do they call? How "loyal" are they?

- Which of my customers require the most technical support? When? What is the pattern?

- What is the technical support call volume forecast for the summer months?

Once this sort of analytical functionality has been implemented, it is not difficult to imagine how the system might evolve into a more active, management control system that allows the client Chief Financial Officer to dial in the following settings:

- Notify me when someone spends more than $100 on a single phone call, $200 in a single day, or $1000 during a given month.

- Send a mail message to any employee whose telecommunications expenses are exceeding the budget we have set for them.

- Provide an automatic monthly report of all international calls of greater than 5 minutes in duration.

- Lock out the following extensions from dialing a given set of area/country codes.

Telecommunications firms can benefit from commercial decision support offerings in the following ways: (a) bundle these services with their basic phone service in order to differentiate their offering and obtain some combination of enhanced rates or market share, (b) sell these services for a fee, since some will be extremely valuable to the customer, and (c) obtain enhanced customer loyalty and "lock-in" by building in enough customizable reporting, analysis, and control features into the system so that the customer does not wish to switch to a new service because the current telecommunication firm's software has become "mission critical" to the customer's own day-to-day operations.

Of course, providing a commercial data warehouse on-line is not without its costs. It may cost tens of millions of dollars or more to provide high concurrency access to massive amounts of data. However, the wisdom of this investment for the telecommunications provider becomes clear when we consider the economics of scale involved. No one can provide a call detail analyzer as cheaply as the provider of the phone service. They have a natural low-cost position in this business, since they can build a particular decision support application (e.g., telecommunications charge-back for a professional services firm) once and then distribute it to tens of thousands of corporations with only slight charges for marginal sales, marketing, and billing expenses. The decision support service becomes just one more line item on a bill that they already send to each of these customers every single month (like selling voicemail packages) and they amortize their development costs over a huge user base.

This sort of success just encourages commercial data warehouse providers to invest more effort in decision support application development and to collect more diverse and greater volumes of data for analysis. Explosive growth is imminent because the value of a data warehouse is proportional to the number of people who query it, the frequency of their queries, and the sophistication of the analysis. As the number of users on the World Wide Web increases, the number of customers for the commercial data warehouse also increases. This results in more revenue to the data warehouse owner, encouraging them to invest in their decision support offerings. As their decision support applications improve, they draw more customers, encourage more frequent usage, and in turn perpetuate this virtuous cycle.

A New Paradigm Emerges

The theme prevalent throughout the present economy is commoditization. In every sector, leading providers are finding that their transactions are losing their differentiation. Consumers can obtain the same services from a variety of banks, insurance firms, ticketing agencies, airlines, hotels, mortgage firms, shipping companies, telecommunications firms, etc. Vendors have their choice of distribution channels, advertising channels, and marketing venues. Retailers are flooded with products, all vying for the same shelf space. Capitalism has been a success, and we are nearly crippled by the number of options presented to us. Emerging from this cacophony of choice is a common strategy across all these lines of business: differentiation through bundled decision support services.

A bank can rise above its competition by providing decision support software that analyzes receipts from customers, payments to suppliers, and asset flows. Health insurance companies can secure the loyalty of a corporate client by providing better expense reporting and therapeutic treatment statistics for area caregivers. A travel agency can provide a system to control costs, analyze business travel patterns, and centrally manage a worldwide travel policy. A consumer packaged goods firm can provide their retail buyer with a category management decision support system, which allows the retailer to obtain a higher rate of returns for that product line. The intended result of these commercial decision support initiatives is a happy customer, leading to more transactions with that customer (i.e., more "shelf-space" and market share).

One useful technique for visualizing the way the world will appear following this transformation is to extrapolate from the example set by automated teller machines (ATMs). ATMs are fairly simple devices, providing rudimentary transaction and decision support services for banks, yet they have become a business necessity for any bank that expects to prosper and grow. A commercial DSS is like a turbo-charged ATM. It can process much more sophisticated transactions, provides rich analytical decision support capabilities, is available in tens of millions of locations, can be upgraded every week if desired, is applicable to nearly every industry, and the core technology is supported by thousands of computer industry vendors and an army of system integrators. For many of us, our only interface with our bank is the ATM. In the future, our primary and perhaps only interface with our vendors may be a software application running over the web, providing data warehouse access and transaction services.

Conclusion

Historically, data warehousing has been a technical initiative in order to control cost or optimize operations. While there are many thousands of internally focused data warehouse initiatives which represent valid IS investments, firms should benefit significantly more over the long term by finding ways to deploy data warehouse access outside of their own employee base to their customers, partners, suppliers, and investors. With the advent of the World Wide Web, the data warehouse is destined to become a profitable, integral part of the revenue-generating function for many firms, contributing to the productivity of millions of knowledge workers.

Notes

Chapter 10

Technology Directions: Toward 2000

—Neal Hill,
Vice President,
Business Intelligence Tools
Cognos, Inc.

Introduction

One of the best know clichés of the information technology industry is, "The only thing constant is change." With the year 2000 rapidly approaching, organizations are starting to think about those changes, as well as the key trends and implications that will be facing them in the new millennium. Objects, virtual reality, Windows NT, data warehousing, the Internet, distributed components, application partitioning, parallel processing: on which trends should an IS manager focus? While many trends can prove fascinating (and perhaps profitable) for a short period of time, the two most likely to prove important over the long term are the Internet and data warehousing.

Data Warehouse: It's More than Just a Storehouse

A data warehouse is a dedicated information system, running parallel to operational systems. Operational systems are the source of the data. The data in the warehouse is organized by subject rather arranged by function. Keeping the end user in mind, a data warehouse is organized for ease of access, user context, and comprehensibility.

A data warehouse provides information to both corporate executives and line managers who are then able to make better decisions and provide better service to their customers. In fact, once a data warehouse is in place, organizations have the option of allowing their customers and/or suppliers to access that data as well.

We are on the verge of a major data warehouse era. While a data warehouse can be a huge strategic advantage in a competitive industry, many companies have yet to actually implement a full-sized data warehouse. Most large companies have at least a small data warehouse project underway. In a survey conducted by Forrester Research in February of 1996, 72% of large companies say that they now have— or will have within 12 months— a data warehouse in place. But according to Meta Group studies, seventy percent of these projects have less than 100 users— and 68% hold less than 50GB of data.

So why is data warehouse so important? It all comes down to the business structure. A traditional business structure has information flowing in and up the organization. Decisions, command, and control flow back down. Due to competitive pressure, today's businesses are pushing decision-making authority back down the organizational chart, empowering knowledge workers at every level. Decision makers need to make better decisions, faster. With the technology now available to create a data warehouse faster, cheaper, and more easily, many end users see a data warehouse as the light at the end of the tunnel.

However, the data warehouse by itself is not the true objective of a data warehouse project. How the data warehouse is used is the key. Beware the end user who "wants a data warehouse." Instead, look to the end user who understands the business needs that a data warehouse can fulfill. IS must understand what the business needs of the end users are, how to design and build multi-source databases, and how to match the organization's requirements with the plethora of end user access tools available on the market today.

IS also needs to carefully plan their data warehouse implementation strategy. Jumping right into a data warehouse project can be a disaster. The way the market is moving, the best method is to start work immediately on a pilot project and roll out complete deployment next year. If you already have your pilot project going, congratulations! You've got a leg up on the competition.

The Internet: What is it...Really?

Other than the computer industry buzzword that has exploded on the mass market, the Internet refers to a "network of networks." It is a text-based environment, with graphics found on the World Wide Web. The Internet brings much more to the party than simply the access to a world-spanning network. It is the embodiment of "Information Everywhere." It is an operating/processing platform with the potential to change how companies distribute information.

The Internet is presently made up of "emaciated clients" (browser software), talking to "hefty servers" (Web servers). However, these browsers are almost always running on a full-scale PC, which represents another, "fatter" client. And database servers are increasingly being connected to Web servers to provide information. Thus, the resulting operating platform model is likely to be "client-client/server-server."

Usage on the 'Net is exploding. Various industry estimates call for more than half a million servers on the Internet by 1997, up from a mere 200 thousand at the end of 1996. And although some estimates have numbered total end users at more than 35 million, current hard data indicates that the number was about 18 million early in 1996, with 60 percent of them in the U.S. Registered commercial domains (Internet addresses that end with .com, indicating a commercial site) jumped 62 percent in the first quarter of 1996 alone.

The Internet is today primarily used for recreational, educational, and entertainment purposes. Data and information is distributed and consumed across the 'Net. Only 11 percent of users ever use their browsers for shopping or buying.

So why is the Internet so important for corporate entities if only a small percentage of people are using it to purchase goods? To find the answer one must examine the tenets of the Information Age. The Internet can supply easy access to information. (We discussed this driver when we discussed data warehousing.) For businesses, there is the possibility of cost-effective, platform-independent distribution and processing of data. This is in addition to the Internet being the first true "universal application" or, as some have deemed it, "history's largest trivia game." Nowhere else can you find such a mass market grouped together, sampling the same wares.

Call it "The Revenge of the Server," but the coming of this new "information everywhere" age will actually result in a resurgence of the importance of servers. Why? Because these sprawling new networks will require strong, well-managed servers to act as control platforms. Another outcome: as the Internet becomes more popular, business cycle times will accelerate, because the universal availability and exchange of information will allow decisions to be made faster. On the technical side, different skills will become valuable as the world turns toward a new platform. Tried to hire an HTML programmer lately? How about someone experienced in TCP/IP, or a network manager? These skills are at the top of everyone's wish list. But technical skills are not the only necessity. Don't forget that all-important "understanding the end user's business needs."

We will also begin to see a reincarnation of the MIS (using that "M" to designate a management position) department— but in a new role. MIS departments will become infrastructure builders and managers, standards-setters, and enablers of our implementation role. No longer will the IS department be relegated to a mere implementation role. And, this new role isn't far off. Over the next year we will see experimentation in data distribution, with 2 - 3 years out for implementation of true distributed processing.

So, What Can You Do Now?

There are huge payoffs in sight. Those who recognize and meet the challenges that lie over the horizon will reap the rewards. IS should look to vendor partners who understand both data access and reporting as well as the potential of the Internet. One without the other will provide a lopsided picture of the future.

Appendix A

Using an Index to Target Customers

—Red Brick Systems

Introduction

Red Brick Systems' TARGETindex™ technology, fully integrated into the Red Brick Warehouse product, specifically addresses the selective identification phase of complex data warehouse queries.

One of the development design goals of TARGETindex was to completely integrate it into the RDBMS engine in all aspects. This includes integration with the data load subsystem, storage and retrieval subsystem, computational subsystem, optimizer, and the serial and parallel execution subsystems.

Other RDBMS approaches to handling selective identification are not well integrated into the core RDBMS engine. Often sold as separate, bolt-on options, other index approaches are limited in their ability to be updated as data is loaded into the warehouse and, in some cases, they store data redundantly. Another weakness is a lack of integration with advanced join processing technology that limits the type of queries that can benefit in a dynamic business environment.

Let's look again at the example query introduced in Chapter 8, *Targeted Marketing and the Data Warehouse*:

```
SELECT customer_id, sum(dollars)
FROM customer_table a,
facts b, products c, time d
WHERE gender = male AND
income_category = HIGH AND
education_level = MASTERS
AND zip_code = 95032 AND
product = "Baseballs" AND
period = "Spring" AND
a.id = b.id AND b.prod = c.prod
AND d.id = b.id;
```

Using TARGETindex, the query would be evaluated in three phases:

- Constraint evaluation

- Join processing

- The net result

Phase 1: Constraint evaluation

During this phase, TARGETindexes created on each of the attributes (gender, income_category, education_level, and zip_code) are processed simultaneously using very efficient bit arithmetic, known as the bit-vectored index approach.

A bit-vectored index maintains information about matching rows by tracking each unique column value in a compact, bit representation. When several keys are being constrained simultaneously, bit representations can be superimposed to form one master bit-vector. This superimposition of multiple indexes is far more computationally efficient and does not entail several byte compares for a single record. Additionally, a very useful by-product is the ability to perform "quick counts" of the number of records that satisfy multiple constraints, simply by counting the bits in the master bit vector.

This technique eliminates unnecessary traversal of the long customer list in our example. Significant performance benefits are realized because I/O and CPU resource usage is minimized and multiple attributes are searched simultaneously.

Phase 2: Join processing

Once the constraints are evaluated, table join processing is accomplished using Red Brick's STARindex in combination with Red Brick's STARjoin™ algorithm. Complete details on this approach can be found in the Red Brick white paper, *Star Schemas and STARjoin Technology*. Contact information is found in *About the Contributors* at the back of this book.

Phase 3: The net result

The net result in this example is extremely fast response times due to the balance and integration of TARGETindex and STARindex.

Performance Analysis—Benchmarks

Holiday Inn Worldwide beta test results

Holiday Inn Worldwide uses Red Brick Warehouse VPT 4.0 to analyze its frequent customer data to develop new marketing programs. By using TARGETindex, the company can quickly segment its customers and design very targeted promotions to improve customer service, revenue and profitability.

Holiday Inn conducted its analysis against a large customer dimensional table containing 5.73 million customer records.

The beta tests were performed on a 125-gigabyte data warehouse running on a uniprocessor IBM RS/6000 model 990 at the customer site. *For more information, see Scenario A.*

"CARS" database benchmark results

In order to validate the performance assumptions of the TARGETindex, a hypothetical "CARS" workload was analyzed. This workload was comprised of analyzing car purchase patterns based on a number of "demographic attributes," and car "properties."

The CARS workload was based on a customer table containing 10 million customers and 25 attributes.

A typical set of 20 queries was run on this database on a Sun SPARCserver 2100 with eight processors. Query speedups ranged from 6x to 74x, with an average space savings of two-thirds of the B-tree space (ranging from 3/4 to 1/2), while index creation speedup ranged from 2x-3x. *For more information, see Scenario B.*

Scenario A

Overview

Red Brick Warehouse VPT 4.0 is the first RDBMS to have fully integrated bit-mapped indexing technology, called TARGETindex. This technology provides functionality critical to deploying customer-centric data warehouse applications. TARGETindex enables data warehouse applications to rapidly segment large and wide customer tables based on targeted customer traits, such as gender, occupation, education level, number of children, and so on. TARGETindex is fully integrated with Red Brick Warehouse and STARindex technology. Once a TARGETindex has been used to select or target a specific customer segment, the STARindex can be used for analysis against this highly-selective customer set.

Application

Holiday Inn Worldwide beta tested Red Brick Warehouse VPT 4.0 for a data warehouse application that analyzes frequent customer data to develop new marketing programs. Using TARGETindex, the company can quickly segment its customers and design targeted promotions to improve customer service, revenue, and profitability. Holiday Inn conducted its analysis against a very large customer table which contained 5.73 million customer records.

Results

Table 1 summarizes the results of a representative set of queries designed to segment a large customer table by income, education, family size, business or pleasure traveler, frequent flyer member, and so on. The indexing methodologies tested for this application included B-tree index and TARGETindex. The results reflect the performance improvement factors for TARGETindex.

Table 1. Results

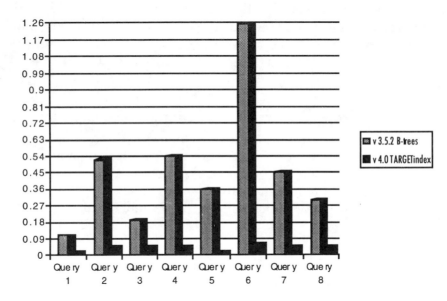

Scenario B

Overview

The "CARS" hypothetical workload was created specifically to analyze the performance benefits that can be realized by using TARGETindex (bit-mapped index). The results clearly demonstrate the efficacy of TARGETindex and its feasibility for these kinds of applications.

In order to stress aspects of the system that are intrinsically unsuitable for traditional indexes, this hypothetical workload was based on a very large, 10 million row, "customer" table with 25 attributes. This simulation of the magnitude of rows and the number of attributes were found to be representative of real-life application situations. The key performance metric in this environment is the ability to selectively identify a subset of the records based on the constraint of several of the attributes. In order to simulate realistic distributions of these attributes, they were artificially generated to reflect the skew that exists in the real world.

Database

The customer table consisted of 10 million, and had 25 attributes. These 25 attributes are described in Table 2. The table contains distribution information regarding the various attributes to reflect reality.

Table 2. Attribute Description Information

Attribute	Description	Domain	Data Type	Distribution
cseq	Customer ID	10 million	int	unique
maker	Auto maker	26	char(20)	Normal
carOrigin	Origin of car	2	char(20)	Normal
types	Type of car	9	char(1)	Normal
door2	2 door vehicle	2	char(1)	65%
door4	4 door vehicle	2	char(1)	35%
sunroof	Sun roof	2	char(1)	25%
convert	Convertible	2	char(1)	15%
alarm	Alarm equipped	2	char(1)	30%
stereo	Stereo equipped	2	char(1)	90%
cd	CD player	2	char(1)	25%
airCond	Air conditioned	2	char(1)	40%
whlDr4	4 wheel drive	2	char(1)	10%
color	Color	13	char(20)	Normal
prCat	Price category	5	int	Exponential
income	Purchaser's income	8	int	Normal (3 mean)
ageGr	Age group	6	int	Normal (3.5 mean)
geoReg	Geographic region	7	char(20)	Normal
ethOrg	Ethnic origin	5	char(20)	Uniform
numHouse	Number in household	9	int	Normal (3.5 mean)
numCars	Number of cars owned	7	int	Normal (2 mean)
gender	Gender	2	char(1)	52%M, 48%F
statekey	State	50	int	Normal
zip	Zip code	22500	int	Normal
yyymm	Birthday	768	int	(1915-1978)

TARGETindex, by virtue of its ability to support the spectrum of domains, is flexible enough to support all the attributes of the customer table.

Table 3 describes the type of TARGETindex created.

Table 3. TARGETindex Types For The Various Attributes

Attributes	Description	TARGETindex
maker	Auto maker	Small
carOrigin	Origin of car	Small
types	Type of car	Small
door2	2 door vehicle	Small
door4	4 door vehicle	Small
sunroof	Sun roof	Small
convert	Convertible	Small
alarm	Alarm equipped	Small
stereo	Stereo equipped	Small
cd	CD player	Small
airCond	Air conditioned	Small
whlDr4	4 wheel drive	Small
color	Color	Small
prCat	Price category	Small
income	Income of purchaser	Small
ageGr	Age group	Small
geoReg	Geographic region	Small
ethOrg	Ethnic origin	Small
numHouse	Number in household	Small
numCars	Number of cars owned	Small
gender	Gender	Small
statekey	State	Medium
zip	Zip code	B-tree
yyymm	Birthday	Medium

Queries

The following queries were designed and used to reflect the query environment that exists in "customer-centric" analysis applications. They were chosen to reflect variations common in these environments:

- Continual incremental constraints to isolate behavioral patterns

- Random incremental constraints to detect potential causal factors

For each of these queries, metrics were collected for speedup associated with the TARGETindex. Additionally, index space efficiency and index creation speeds were measured to illustrate "other" implicit benefits associated with integrating new bit-mapped technology with an already efficient engine infrastructure.

```
/* cars-q101
```
How many cars were bought by women in age group greater than or equal to three, with income greater than or equal to three, and who live in the west? */

```
select 'q101-paw3',
       count(*)
               from cars
               where gender = 'F'
               and agegr >= 3
               and income >= 3
               and georeg = 'west'
;
```

```
/* cars-q102
```
How many domestic cars were bought by women with age group greater than or equal to three, income greater than or equal to three, and who live in the west? */

```
select 'q102-paw3',
       count(*)
               from cars
               where gender = 'F'
               and      agegr >= 3
               and      income >= 3
               and      georeg = 'west'
               and      carorigin = 'domestic'
;
```

/* cars-q103
How many Chevrolet cars were bought by women with age group greater than or equal to three, income great than or equal to three, and who live in the west? */

```
select  'q103-paw3',
        count(*)
                from cars
                where gender = 'F'
                and    agegr >= 3
                and    income >= 3
                and    georeg = 'west'
                and    maker = 'chevrolet'
;
```

/* cars-q104
How many Chevrolet cars of type sports utility were bought by women with age group greater than or equal to three, income greater than or equal to three, and live in the west? */

```
select  'q104-paw3',
        count(*)
                from cars
                where gender = 'F'
                and    agegr >= 3
                and    income >= 3
                and    georeg = 'west'
                and    maker = 'chevrolet'
                and    types = 'sports utility'
;
```

/* cars-q105
How many Chevrolet cars of type sports utility and with two doors were
bought by women with age group greater than or equal to three, income
greater than or equal to three, and who live in the west? */

```
select 'q105-paw3',
       count(*)
       from cars
       where gender = 'F'
            and    agegr >= 3
            and    income >= 3
            and    georeg = 'west'
            and    maker = 'chevrolet'
            and    types = 'sports utility'
            and    door2 = 'Y'
;
```

/* cars-q106
How many white, 2 door, Chevrolet, sports utility cars were bought by
women with age group greater than or equal to three, income greater than
or equal to three but less than or equal to four, and who live in the west? */

```
select 'q106-paw3',
       count(*)
            from cars
            where gender = 'F'
            and    agegr >= 3
            and    (income >= 3 or income <= 4)
            and    georeg = 'west'
            and    maker = 'chevrolet'
            and    types = 'sports utility'
            and    door2 = 'Y'
            and    color = 'white'
;
```

/* cars-q107
How many white, 2-door, type sports utility, Chevrolet cars were bought
by women with age group greater than or equal to three, income greater
than or equal to three but less than or equal to four, and who live in the
west? */

```
select 'q107-paw3',
       count(*)
              from cars, states
              where gender = 'F'
              and    agegr >= 3
              and    (income >= 3 or income <= 4)
              and    maker = 'chevrolet'
              and    types = 'sports utility'
              and    door2 = 'Y'
              and    color = 'white'
              and    georeg = 'west'
              and    numhouse >= 2
;
```

/* cars-q108
How many white, 2-door, type sports utility, Chevrolet cars were bought
by women with age group greater than or equal to three, income greater
than or equal to three but less than or equal to four, where households
have two or more, and who live in the west in the state of California? */

```
select 'q108-paw3',
       count(*)
              from cars, states
              where gender = 'F'
              and    agegr >= 3
              and    (income >= 3 or income <= 4)
              and    maker = 'chevrolet'
              and    types = 'sports utility'
              and    door2 = 'Y'
              and    color = 'white'
              and    georeg = 'west'
              and    numhouse >= 2
              and    state = 'california'
;
```

/* cars-q109
How many sports utility vehicles were bought with 4 wheel drive
option?*/

```
select 'q109-paw3',
        count(*)
                from cars
                where types = 'sports utility'
                and    whldr4 = 'Y'
;
```

/* cars-q110
How many compact cars with 2 doors were bought by households with
two or more, and price category = 2? */

```
select 'q110-paw3',
        count(*)
                from cars
                where types = 'compact'
                and    door2 = 'Y'
                and    numhouse <= 2
                and    prcat = 2
;
```

/* cars-q111
How many midsize sedans with 4 doors were bought by households with
four, and price category >= 3 with income group 4?*/

```
select'q111-paw3',
        count(*)
                from cars
                where types = 'midsize sedan'
                and    door4 = 'Y'
                and    numhouse = 4
                and    prcat >= 3
                and    income = 4
;
```

```
/* cars-q112
How many Bentley cars were bought by people in age group four and
income greater than or equal to four? */
select'q112-paw3',
        count(*)
                from cars
                where maker = 'bentley'
                and     income >= 4
                and     agegr = 4
;


/* cars-q113
How many Porsches were sold to women with income = 3, lives in
Florida, and has birthday between 1960-1965? */
select 'q113-paw3',
        count(*)
                from cars, states
                where maker = 'porsche'
                and     income = 3
                and     state = 'florida'
                and     yyyymm between 196001 and 196512
;


/* cars-q114
How many cars were sold to households with income greater than 80K
and live in the west? */
select 'q114-paw3',
        count(*)
                from cars
                where income >= 5
                and     georeg = 'west'
;


/* cars-q115
How many cars were sold to households with income greater than 80K
and live in California?   */
select 'q115-paw3',
        count(*)
                from cars, states
                where income >= 5
                and     state = 'california'
;
```

```
/* cars-q116
How many cars were sold to Hispanic households with income greater
than 80K and live in California?   */
select 'q116-paw3',
        count(*)
                from cars, states
                where income >= 5
                and    state = 'california'
                and    ethorg = 'hispanic'
;
```

```
/* cars-q117
How many mini-vans were sold to men in age group 3, in price category
2, and with a household of two? */
select 'q117-paw3',
        count(*)
                from cars
                where types = 'mini-van'
                where agegr = 3
                and    gender = 'M'
                and    prcat = 2
                and    numhouse = 2
;
```

```
/* cars-q118
How many large-size sedans in the third price category were bought by
people with income equal to four and who already have two cars at home?
*/
select 'q118-paw3',
        count(*)
                from cars
                where types = 'largesize sedan'
                and    prcat = 3
                and    income = 4
                and    numcars = 2
;
```

/* cars-q119
How many pink 4-door Cadillacs were sold?*/

```
select 'q119-paw3',
       count(*)
              from cars
              where maker = 'cadillac'
              and    color = 'pink'
              and    door4 = 'Y'
;
```

/* cars-q120
How many Toyota convertible cars were bought by people with a zipcode
between 80000 and 81000? */

```
select 'q120-paw3',
       count(*)
              from cars
              where maker = 'toyota'
              and    convert = 'Y'
              and zip between 80000 and 81000
;
```

Results

Query speedups from 6x to 74x were experienced. TARGETindex integration provides unparalleled performance improvements for these selective identification applications. Customer-centric applications will require database engines to manifest performance conducive to iterative attribute-oriented investigation.

Table 4 summarizes the query times and speedups experienced.

Table 4. Query Times and Speedups— v3.5 vs v4.0

Query	v3.5	v4.0	Speedup
q101	206	9	23x
q102	236	7	35x
q103	181	4	41x
q104	260	4	61x
q105	282	5	62x
q106	415	6	73x
q107	452	8	57x
q108	450	13	36x
q109	34	3	12x
q110	105	2	51x
q111	132	2	53x
q112	502	2	22x
q113	44	4	12x
q114	18	6	3x
q115	43	6	7x
q116	98	2	51x
q117	110	2	68x
q118	43	1	39x
q119	30	1	27x

TARGETindexes also were designed with space optimization as an objective. The benefits of this design are evident from the space reductions which ranged from 5x to 104x based on distribution and density.

Table 5 summarizes space reductions experienced by virtue of TARGETindexes.

Table 5. Index Space Reduction Using TARGETindexes

Index Name	v3.5 Index size (KB)	v4.0 Index size (KB)	Index Shrinkage
maker	261759	32256	8x
carOrigin	261759	2512	104x
types	261759	11192	23x
door2	70288	2496	28x
door4	70288	2496	28x
sunroof	70288	2496	28x
convert	70288	2496	28x
alarm	70288	2496	28x
stereo	70288	2496	28x
cd	70288	2496	28x
airCond	70288	2496	28x
whlDr4	70288	2496	28x
color	261759	16152	16x
prCat	100418	6208	16x
income	100418	9920	10x
ageGr	100418	7448	13x
geoReg	261759	7472	35x
ethOrg	261759	6224	42x
numHouse	100418	7448	13x
numCars	100418	7448	13x
gender	70288	2496	28x
statekey	100418	1186	48x
yyymm	100418	22080	5x

While traditional bit-mapped implementations have somewhat improved query performance, they have been prohibitively slow in index creation as part of load processing. TARGETindex by design was based on the legacy of superior performance offered by Red Brick Warehouse.

Table 6 summarizes index creation speedups which ranged from 2x to 5x when compared with traditional B-tree indexes for the same attributes.

Table 6. Index Creation Speedups Using TARGETindexes

Index Name	v3.5 Creation time	v4.0 Creation time	Speedup
maker	2047	624	3x
carOrigin	2440	539	5x
types	1950	557	4x
door2	1116	557	2x
door4	1302	560	2x
sunroof	1358	551	2x
convert	1326	556	2x
alarm	1481	556	3x
stereo	1091	561	2x
cd	1247	562	2x
whlDr4	1193	560	2x
airCond	1154	566	2x
color	2169	573	4x
prCat	1681	554	3x
income	1952	697	3x
ageGr	1312	565	2x
geoReg	2695	617	4x
ethOrg	2525	554	5x
numHouse	2220	566	4x
numCars	1839	557	3x
gender	1731	641	3x
statekey	1431	643	2x
yyymm	1621	501	2x

In summary, TARGETindexes are optimal for this class of selective identification applications.

Appendix B

Evaluating an Advanced Indexing Technology

—Lois Richards,
Data Warehousing Product Manager,
Dynamic Information Systems Corporation

Introduction

How should you evaluate an indexing product? This is a list of required features that any Advanced Indexing product should provide.

Keyword retrievals. Index should allow selection of records or entries based on the content of the data (any keyword or numeric value in a string of text, date or quantity).

Qualifying counts. Index should automatically provide instant qualification counts. Users can immediately find out how many records qualify for a given query. Qualifying counts allow queries to be further qualified, expanded, or discarded if the results were unsatisfactory, without touching the database itself.

Complex searches. Index should support multiple column and multiple table criteria searches, Boolean and relational logic (and, or, not, greater than, less than, equal to, etc.), multiple table joins, partial keys, ranges, and drill-down (iterative) searches.

Index-only capabilities. Index should perform functions such as qualifying counts, drill-down searches and summarizations without accessing the underlying data structures. Eliminate unnecessary disk I/O's.

Aggregation indexes. Index should support fast arithmetic calculations of data values.

Case insensitive. Index should locate textual data with or without upper and lower case matching.

Pattern matching. Index should allow partially specified arguments to be used to query data. Full data value entries are not required.

Soundex. Index should support phonetic search of data.

Composite keywording. Index should be able to concatenate columns or select bytes within columns.

Grouping of Columns. Index should allow columns to be grouped into one logical retrieval unit. For example, columns ADDRESS1, ADDRESS2, ADDRESS3 could be grouped together to allow users to easily retrieve on city, state or address information, regardless of which column the data is located.

Pre-joined Indexing. Index should be able to combine the indexes for columns from more than one table. This allows fast cross-table joins for retrievals that select from columns in more than one table.

Ease design process. Index should build and store indexes in a structure separate, independent of the underlying structure. There should be no need for structural changes. This supports the storage of more detail data. By keeping more detail, users can query virtually anything in the data warehouse and not be limited by pre-defined summarization tables.

Fast retrieval speeds. Index should be able to qualify records at speeds up to 1 million records per second, providing fast answers to users' questions.

Fast, efficient indexing. Index should build indexes at speeds of up to 100 million keywords per hour. Indexes should also employ a compression technology for efficiency in data storage.

Portability. A flexible indexing technology should support access and retrieval of data stored in differing databases and file systems on several platforms.

Notes

About the Contributors

The following expert-solutions companies contributed to this book:

- *Cognos, Inc.*
- *Dynamic Information Systems Corporation (DISC)*
- *MicroStrategy, Inc.*
- *NCR, Inc.*
- *PLATINUM technology, inc.*
- *Praxis International Inc.*
- *Prism Solutions, Inc.*
- *Red Brick Systems, Inc.*

Cognos, Inc.

Chapter 10, Technology Directions: Toward 2000

Cognos, Inc.
67 South Bedford Street
Burlington, MA 01803-5164
www.cognos.com
tel: 617-229-6600
fax: 617-229-9844
info@cognos.com

Dynamic Information Systems Corporation

Chapter 7, Bringing Performance to Your Data Warehouse
Appendix B, Evaluating an Advanced Indexing Technology

Dynamic Information Systems Corporation (DISC)
5733 Central Avenue
Boulder, CO, 80301
www.disc.com
tel: 303-444-4000
fax: 303-444-7460
info@disc.com

MicroStrategy, Inc.

Chapter 5, The Case for Relational OLAP

Chapter 9, Paradigm Shattered: How the Web Will Redefine the Role of the Data Warehouse

MicroStrategy, Inc.

8000 Towers Crescent Drive

Vienna, VA 22182

www.strategy.com

tel: 703-848-8600

fax: 703-848-8610

info@strategy.com

Michael J. Saylor, author of *Paradigm Shattered: How the Web Will Redefine the Role of the Data Warehouse,* Chapter 9 in this book, is the Founder, President and CEO of MicroStrategy, Inc., which supplies the DSS Agent Relational OLAP product and the DSS Web tool for use with Internet browsers. Prior to founding the company in 1989, he worked at E.I. du Pont de Nemours & Co., where he was involved in efforts to apply simulation and database technology to strategic planning. Mr. Saylor can be reached by e-mail at: saylor@strategy.com

NCR, Inc.

Chapter 1, The Heart of the Data Warehouse

NCR, Inc.
17095 Via Del Campo
San Diego, CA 92127
www.ncr.com
tel: 619-485-2716
fax: 619-485-3540

Chapter 4, Building Decision Support Systems for Quick ROI

PLATINUM *technology, inc.*
1815 South Meyers Road
Oakbrook Terrace, IL 60181
www.platinum.com
tel: 630-620-5000
    800-442-6861
fax: 630-691-0710
info@platinum.com

PLATINUM *technology, inc.* helps businesses manage and improve software operations. Headquartered in the Chicago suburb of Oakbrook Terrace, Illinois, PLATINUM distributes its products worldwide through a network of domestic and international sales offices, resellers, and systems integrators. Additional information about PLATINUM *technology, inc.* is available via the World Wide Web site at http://www.platinum.com, or call 1-800-442-6861 or 1-630-620-5000.

Praxis International Inc.

Chapter 3, Selecting a Data Replicator

Praxis International Inc.
245 Winter Street
Waltham, MA 02154-8716
www.praxisint.com
tel: 617-622-5751
fax: 617-622-5766
praxis@praxisint.com

Prism Solutions, Inc.

Chapter 2, Paving the Way to Data Warehouse Project Success

Prism Solutions, Inc.
1000 Hamlin Court
Sunnyvale, CA 94089
www.prismsolutions.com
tel: 408-752-1888
fax: 408-752-1875
info@prismsolutions.com

Red Brick Systems, Inc.

Chapter 6, Specialized Requirements for Relational Data Warehouse Servers
Chapter 8, Targeted Marketing and the Data Warehouse
Appendix A, Using an Index to Target Customers

Red Brick Systems, Inc.
485 Alberto Way
Los Gatos, CA 95032
www.redbrick.com
tel: 800-777-2585
fax: 408-399-3277
info@redbrick.com

Notes